M000309176

A Gradual Redemption

A Gradual Redemption

A story of faith,
choice and the
sovereignty of God

Kelly A. Williams

A Gradual Redemption: A story of faith, choice and the sovereignty of God

Copyright © by Kelly A. Williams. All rights reserved.

ISBN: 978-0-615-49900-0 (Paperback Edition)
ISBN: 978-0-9883452-2-5 (Kindle Edition)
Library of Congress Control Number: 2011937960

No part of this publication may be reproduced, stored in a retrieval system or transmitted in any way by any means, electronic, mechanical, photocopy, recording or otherwise without the prior permission of the author, except as provided by USA copyright law.

All Scripture quotations, unless otherwise indicated, are taken from the New King James Version. Copyright © 1982 by Thomas Nelson, Inc. Used by permission. All rights reserved.

Published by Air In Motion Publishers, LLC.
1963 Clark Road | Indianapolis, IN 46224 USA
A Division of Air In Motion Ministries, LLC
www.airinmotionministries.com

Cover and interior design: Suzanne Parada
Editor: Janet Schwind
Photography: Rick McIntyre

ACKNOWLEDGMENTS

I'm not exactly sure how to begin to thank, or at least acknowledge, every person who helped bring this endeavor to pass. Perhaps, because God always starts with what He has, it's best to start at the beginning of the journey.

To God's prophets (Tavio, Irma, Barbara and Tom) who, out of their obedience to the Lord, spoke an anointed word to me at just the appointed time that cast God's vision and truly guided me through every step along the way. My gratitude goes beyond measure or expression.

To my mother, the one who without exception has been there since my very first breath. Your strength and courage have been an unbelievable model of inspiration and without it, I would have never journeyed from the cave. Thank you for the freedom to tell the story no matter the cost it may bring to you. I'll be forever grateful that I got to be your daughter— thank you for *everything*.

To my husband, my partner, not only in life but in the Spirit. What a ride it has been, no? Words alone cannot do justice to the role you have played in my life and in this story. For every time you led the way, for every tear you cried with me, and for every burden you have helped me carry, thank you. This book would not exist if not for your unwavering faith and support, let alone your listening ear. Thank you for staying in the delivery room with me; you're an unbelievable "coach" and I'm so excited to see where God takes us.

To my children, Matthew, Anna, and Aaron: Wow! How many times I have stood back and marveled at your hearts for the Lord. You each, in your own individual ways, have encouraged, listened, inspired, supported, and helped bear the weight of the past ten months. Matthew, your zeal, passion and vision have been an invaluable source of inspiration, particularly when I wasn't sure I would cross the finish line. Thank you for having faith and continually casting vision, especially during the hardest of days.

Anna, your tenacity and quiet strength have been a bedrock of support. Those summer porch conversations that brought about so much confirmation have continually reminded me that this project was God's heart for our family. Words fail to express my gratitude for your insight and attention to the different manuscripts, and how with such clarity you helped strengthen my voice so the reader would better understand the journey. Thank you for hearing so clearly and praying so diligently— you are our own personal wrecking ball.

To my Aaron, your sensitivity and tenderness throughout the process was unparalleled. On the most difficult days you were the one who somehow knew to call and ask just the right questions, then listen so faithfully as I tried to process what God was taking me through. Thank you for sharing the weight of the burden. Your timeliness and insight helped me persevere.

To Richard, Cheryl, Lauren and Jim: Thank you for the years of countless laughter and tears. Thank you for the moments of spoken truth and steadfast support. And Jim, for the heart to consistently check on me and pray without ceasing, thank you. You truly fill the shoes that were left empty so very long ago.

Janet, God brought you in at the very last hour (surprised?), and I couldn't be more thankful. Not only did He bring me an invaluable editor, He brought me an incredible new friend whom I can't wait to journey with and explore God's heart together. For every revision, suggestion and connection, THANK YOU; you made the process SO much easier.

To the countless others: John, an incredible source of unconditional and unwavering love. You are truly one of us, and there's nowhere else you belong. To Jo (my biggest cheerleader and visualist), Lori, Tammy and the CCHS family: for every piece of encouragement, every moment celebrated and every tear cried, oh how I thank you. Only God knows how deep and how wide my love and appreciation go for every one of you.

Lastly, to Jesus: I have no words. May every letter, every word, every sentence, every paragraph and every chapter reflect my love and gratitude for You and You alone. Thank You for choosing me and for pulling me out from the rubble. You are the one true God—may my story be a reflection of that truth. Thank You for the opportunity; it's been an unspeakable honor. Τετέλεσται

FOREWORD

Story has a powerful way of impacting how we see life. Revelation 12:11 states that they were saved by the blood of Christ and "the word of their testimony," implying there is something profound that occurs when we talk about what God is doing in our midst. Maybe because when we share what God is doing we copy the example that God has given us—He told His story with Israel in the Old Testament. So when we tell our stories we cannot help but ultimately tell of a God who is faithfully operating behind the scenes in our lives. Every time we talk about our lives, we end up revealing the process the Lord has us on in the midst of our circumstances. We may never say the name of God, but He is constant. We cannot help but unwittingly tell of this God whose main desire is not to punish us or to tell us how bad we are, but rather to love us into transformation. In practical ways hearing someone's story immediately draws us into reflection on our own. When a story is told, and told well, there are things we discover about ourselves that can revolutionize how we see life.

The story that is being conveyed in *A Gradual Redemption*—while about God's redemption of a situation and ultimately His glory in a submitted life—is even more than that; it is the story of discovering God's heart for His daughter. What this book captures is the picture of a God who is yearning to bring about restoration. A God who can take any situation presented and bring wonderful redemption in the midst of heartache and despair. Not just redemption of circumstances—that comes in time—but ultimately, redemption in a relationship with Him.

This story begins with the choices of a typical teenage girl caught up in things above her maturity level. The particular story is one that resonates with many of our experiences because it is a story of rebellion, the story of loss of innocence, the story of surrendering what is rightfully ours. The difference is that as Kelly's story unfolds, she not only experiences redemption but perhaps equally important, she acquires a language for the process of redemption through which God takes her—and all of us. She paints a picture of what it looks like when King David's "O Lord, you have searched me and known me" transpires (Psalm 139:1).

The nature of Kelly's particular story is that she, like so many, was caught in the midst of her rebellion to God. And where one would expect to find frustration and anger from the Lord, it becomes a story capturing snapshots in time of God's gentleness and His heart to love His people—even when they rebel against that love. It's a depiction of a God who yearns for relationship with His people. The picture of a God who is *quick* to show mercy and grace. The story of a God who doesn't require His children to be afraid of Him, but rather to be empowered with confidence that the love He demonstrates *to* them and *for* them can overcome any situation they find themselves in. God's statement about Himself is, "...I have satiated the weary soul, and I have replenished every sorrowful soul" (Jer. 31:25). Above all, God's heart is to bring rest and peace to all of His children, and to bring reconciliation to the areas where we have given something of ourselves over to the enemy. There is nothing outside the realm of possibility—no story too grave, no decision too destructive, no life too lost. God is the Great Redeemer. And while the redemption may not be overnight, the Lord's heart is *always* to bring redemption to His children.

—Matthew J. Williams

"And they overcame him by the
blood of the Lamb and by the word
of their testimony, and they did not
love their lives to the death."

Revelation 12:11

CHAPTER ONE

Defining Moments

ABOVE ALL ELSE it's the look in his eyes I remember. Not his bandaged, unshaven face, nor his medicinal smell that can still penetrate my nostrils if I allow myself to linger in the memorialized living room of my toddler home. I was three and it was Easter morning. My mother had dressed my sisters and me in the traditional Easter chiffon of most young Catholic girls, complete with white gloves and hats and the infamous black patent leather shoes shined to their optimum brilliance. I desperately wanted to twirl so my dress would flow out as the air got caught up underneath it, but instead I stood before him fidgeting, fighting to stand still. He was hard to look at yet it was all I wanted to do. His eyes were kind though his bandaged face frightened me. I didn't understand at the time how sick he was for I was too young, and I certainly hadn't yet developed the sense for picking up on the tension that hung in the room caused by his drunken behavior. I just wanted to twirl for my father because in his eyes I would discover my own beauty, regardless of his stitched up face and rank smell.

He was slouched, almost bent in half, as if it hurt him to sit erect, and my attention was drawn to the moving bandage on the right side of his mouth as he softly asked the three of us to, "Turn around, I want to see you."

I remember that twirl and what it felt like to hear him say, "You look beautiful," then my memory fades, leaving behind the lingering feeling of how completely satisfied I felt in his presence—even at three.

The second and last memory I have occurs barely two months later. Again disheveled and unshaven, he now sits on a different couch—my grandmother's, his mother, while I sit at his feet and play before two of my favorite men: my father and his brother. I can still hear his voice, weary and nearly broken down as he argues with his mother about shaving. He wasn't ready to get up. "I will, I will," he reluctantly repeats. I look up and watch his head fall back and rest on the arch of the couch. He closes his eyes and silently nods as she says, "You're going to be late, Tommy." His only response is a frustrated sounding exhale. I remain at his feet, the warmth of the sun penetrating through the open door, once again enjoying his presence.

I don't remember him getting up yet somehow remember hearing my grandmother tell my uncle, "He can't go to the dentist looking like that," and the next thing that echoes through my memory is the sound of the CRASH that reverberates throughout the trailer. I see the "knowing" looks pass from my uncle to my grandmother and then feel what seems like a ripple of vibration creep across the trailer floor as if carrying the news of impending doom. I shiver as the goose bumps crawl from the small of my back to the base of my skull, cementing an almost four-year-old's awareness that something is deathly wrong.

I have grown up since that day with the knowledge that my father died when he was just 36, caused in large part by extreme alcohol abuse. His autopsy revealed his pancreas, compromised by years of drinking, had exploded, sending a blood clot to his heart. He died instantly that day in my grandmother's bathroom, leaving behind my mother, who had already been widowed once, her three children whom he had loved as his own, as well as two of his blood children—my older brother and me. But what has taken years for me to grasp is the insight into the gaping hole my father's death created in my own heart. The place where I once knew beauty and adoration was left void and vacant, creating a vast expanse of emptiness that I have struggled to contain.

In my younger years, while growing up in northeast Ohio, community and family were all I really knew. I thrived in the sense of belonging that my small town represented—I loved being in relationship and the feeling that came from belonging to a group of people, particularly my social circle. Their acceptance helped make the expanse often go unnoticed. Certainly the unexpected loss of two different fathers helped define the environment of our home, but the specific ramifications of such losses went fairly undetected. The only indicators that existed occurred in the isolated moments when I would watch the role my friends' fathers played in their lives and I could witness their personal interactions. Only then could I remotely acknowledge something was missing because I had no practical understanding of how their father's affection actually made them feel; all I had to draw from were the two memories of a three year old. Most days I was left to wonder how my life would be different if my father had been there to hug me or ask how I was, like their fathers did. I envied their relationships and was always left feeling like an outsider looking in—a window shopper, in a sense. Although able to see what the clothes look like on the mannequin in the store window, I was always left to wonder what they would actually feel like if I ever got to wear them.

Knowing I wasn't the only one who felt the glass partition was a major source of consolation for me. My four siblings and I were all growing up without the reassurance, love and security of our respective fathers; however, what we did have was a strong woman for a mother. From the loss of her first husband in a car accident to the death of my own father, my mother remained steadfast and committed to overcoming; she refused to be defeated. And while not a woman of pronounced faith, we grew up with morals and values because of her constant reinforcement of right and wrong. My mother was strong and courageous, and above all else, loved all of us. And we knew it.

Beyond her being the one consistent presence in my childhood, my mother was the only source of stability for countless reasons. She was the sole counselor, nursemaid, comforter, and disciplinarian of her children, and although she remarried when I was a young girl, he was a father in name only. He seldom engaged with our family unit and most often remained emotionally aloof throughout their marriage. Subsequently, by the time I completed my sophomore year of high school, the demise of their relationship became the impetus for my fairly protected existence to become something altogether different.

CHAPTER TWO

Civil Unrest

I WAS 15 and just beginning my sophomore year of high school when my mother and stepfather decided to live in separate bedrooms. An odd feeling filled the house as I watched both of them navigate through narrow hallways and otherwise empty rooms trying to avoid each other. I never fully understood why he didn't just move out, but the specifics of their decision were never my business so I just learned how to maneuver through the awkwardness. However, by late spring it felt as if the house's atmosphere would self-combust with one wayward glance or an ill-timed word.

With tensions mounting, it shouldn't have come as a surprise that something about the way we were living needed to change; after all, one, or in this case two, can only walk on eggshells for so long before the weight of pressure causes the frail exterior to crack. Therefore, when one of my older sisters called and said she was being transferred to an army base on the east side of Indianapolis, and then a week later a position became available with my mother's employer on the south side of that same city, the situation felt like more than mere coincidence. I remember standing in the kitchen as my mother presented the news that we would be moving, and feeling torn between not wanting to leave my friends and being intimately aware of how unhappy my mother had been. Something deep inside me knew, without really understanding, that we needed to get away from the growing hostility that was consuming the house. So, while I had no desire to leave my school, my friends or my community I conceded to the plan with a half grin, having no concept of what it all actually meant.

I spent the next six weeks wrapping up the details of my life in Ohio with going-away parties, graduation parties, and saying goodbye at family reunions. And even though Indiana was only one state west, most people reacted as if it was half- way around the world. Inevitably I would find myself observing and silently wondering if I'd ever see these people again. As the baby of the family, I had grown quite familiar with the difficulty that accompanied watching my older siblings move away. I had grown to hate the silence that greeted me in place of their laughter and camaraderie, but I had found solace in the companionship of my friends. Without their companionship I wondered who would keep me company. But despite the internal dragging of my feet, June had found its way to our door long before I was truly ready. And after years of family life in a small steel town in northeast Ohio had been successfully packed into a 20-foot U-Haul, my mother drove one state west as I stared out the passenger window and wondered how different life was actually going to be.

Having lived most of my young life in the same house located in the same small town, my feeling of being transplanted was almost immediate. Contrary to my best efforts, I struggled over the summer months to relate to the ease of adaptability I witnessed in the other kids who came from surrounding military families and were used to frequently relocating. Despite the reassurance of both my mother and sister, I remained socially void of any ability to truly engage with peers of my own. Instead, I felt completely uprooted and disconnected from everything familiar and began to struggle more deeply than ever before with my need to belong and be known. The only thing I could see was how different I was from everyone else, which always left me yearning for home where the people were more like me.

The people near me now had lived in various parts of the world, and I only knew a small steel town in the valley. The kids I sat with in school spoke of having sex, drinking and smoking pot while my innocence was still so intact that I wasn't sure I knew how to kiss a boy, let alone relate to the things they were discussing. I soon discovered I virtually had no point of reference to relate to them or their way of life, and I found myself continually trying to silence the internal voices in my head that kept droning, *You don't belong here. You'll never fit in.*

I fought to make sense of my newfound chaos and every day after school for nearly two months, I would trudge my way up the open stairway, resentment mounting with each step taken. I was clearly struggling to come to some kind of terms with my new environment and longed to feel normal again. The wind whipped through the staircase and I watched as the nearby fallen leaves were swept up into what looked like their own mini tornadoes then gradually fell to their new location. *Humph, that's exactly how I feel*, I thought, *swept up and dropped in a place I don't belong.* I dug around for my keys, then continued my ascent, relishing the thought of another school day done and behind me.

It wasn't until I threw the mail on the table that an envelope bearing an Ohio return address caught my attention. Addressed to all three of us, I quickly ripped open the envelope and discovered that we were invited to a November wedding. My spirits rose for the first time in months. "I could go home," I whispered to myself. I sat down and let my mind travel the 400-plus miles that separated me from all I really knew and loved. *Imagine how good it will be to be back*, I told myself, *even if it is just for a weekend.*

Savoring every moment of my upcoming visit only increased the yearning for my former life, and by mid November my mother knew it. Confronting her on a daily basis was the constant misplaced feeling I was living under, compounded by her own desire to reconcile the differences in her marriage. Neither of us were exactly content; therefore, a week before the wedding my mother shared with me that she and my stepfather decided to try and "make it work," and she would be transferring back to Ohio in January with her employer. I tried to contain my excitement as she went on to explain, "Kelly, I know you're not happy, so if you would like to move back next weekend when we go home for the wedding, your stepfather said you can live with him, then just after the New Year I'll move back."

I felt an immediate internal mechanism click and resisted the urge to shout "YES!" as if I had just won an invisible battle. I silently relished the thought of no longer having to listen to the internal voices ostracizing me from any viable social interactions. Instead her declaration was as if an emotional line had been drawn, empowering me to endure the next few weeks of life among strangers without feeling hopeless. I sat back and exhaled as if I had just awoken from a bad dream. "I can go home, really?" I asked my mother. She slowly closed her eyes as she nodded her head in agreement and said, "Yes, Kelly, you can go home."

~~~~~~

Although the house felt oddly different than when we first lived there, I couldn't help but delight in seeing every strategically placed piece of my bedroom furniture back in its rightful place. The color of my room, the plaid carpet, the whistle of the steel mill signifying the 5:00 p.m. quitting time—all indicators that I was exactly where I belonged. I looked out the window and watched as the wind swept the last remnants of leaves off the front oak tree and thought about how difficult it was going to be to say goodbye to my mother. *What will life look like without her?* I wondered.

Don't think about that now, I ordered myself, and instead allowed the thrill of being home again to overshadow my wonderment and diminish my need to prepare for the days ahead when my heart would ache for my mother's physical presence. Turning from the window I looked around and took comfort in the familiar surroundings as I began creating my mental checklist of the friends I would call, believing their companionship would help occupy the time until my mother returned home.

The void my mother's absence created was nearly immediate, and in the few short months I had been in Indiana, I had all but forgotten how silent my family's home had become the past few years. Now more than ever, without her presence there was literally no one to talk to, and I found most of my time spent anticipating our phone conversations or counting the days until Christmas break when my stepfather and I would visit her in Indiana. In the other quiet moments, at night when I lay in bed and allowed my mind the freedom to truly examine my situation, I always came to the same conclusion: life must consist of two evils, and I was fairly confident that I had picked the lesser of the two, for at least in this small town I didn't feel like an outsider.

Knowing Christmas was approaching made the days seem more tolerable until gradually they became weeks, and with each X on the calendar I was slowly establishing my own routine. Certainly some days felt as if they wouldn't pass fast enough, so by the time Christmas arrived I was so excited to see my mother and siblings that I didn't have the sense or the eyes to see anything else during our time together. I just took refuge and relished the familiarity that came from being with family. So when my mother returned to Ohio two weeks later and discussed the state of her union with me, I was fairly surprised at the news that too much relational damage had occurred in her marriage, making the chasm far too wide for either of them to bridge. She went on to explain that after much deliberation my parents had decided it was best if they divorced. Then she grew silent, and I wondered if it was from the sadness I saw written on her face or if she had more to say and was searching for her words.

I watched as she fought to gain her composure and then listened as her voice slowly gained strength with each word she spoke: "Kelly, I've made some hard decisions. Now you're going to have to." Then she paused and just looked at me. I clearly didn't understand until she continued, "I've decided it's better for me to stay in Indianapolis. I'd like you to move back to Indiana with me, but if you want to live here until you graduate, your stepfather said you could."

In a whirlwind of facts and probabilities, my head swirled with indecision as I listened to her. I was well aware that right then I seemed emotionally stable and sure of myself. My grades were good, my friends were reputable, and, on all accounts, I appeared level headed and "mature for my age." What I didn't understand was that choices, whether those personally made or ones made on your behalf, have the potential to forever alter anyone's course. For, while I believed at that moment that staying in Ohio with my friends, secure in their acceptance, would outweigh the negative aspect of not living with my mother, I truly had no viable concept of how much stability and security her daily presence brought me. Certainly at 16 I thought I could handle anything, so it didn't take long for me to decide that weekend fixes and frequent visits from my mother would have to be enough to sustain me. And although subtle doubts pricked at my soul, I dismissed them with the pleasure of familiarity.

~~~~~~

The excitement I had initially felt when I returned to Ohio in November began to slowly dissipate over those cold January days. Living with my stepfather, although it was in my childhood home, was entirely different from anything I had ever known. He worked nights so when I came home from school there was no one there to share a meal or discuss the day's events, and the contrast of living in a home where there had once been abundant life and laughter was increasingly obvious. In the evenings Silence quickly became my sole companion.

Weekends were painfully quiet until I discovered that avoidance is a viable solution to unsolvable dilemmas. My own personal routine quickly began to include as many outings with my friends and their families as possible. It became my way of escaping what would have been an involuntary experiment in solitary confinement. It didn't take long before I realized if I occupied the time with them, my sanity somehow stayed in check; otherwise I would have spent untold hours over the weekends alone and without any life in the house, making it feel like time would never pass. Although my stepfather was home more often than not, he remained conversationally aloof and isolated. We were merely two separate beings existing in the same space—until things began to shift. On nights when I would return home late from being out with friends, his overt physical attention and need for conversation began to register alarm in me. Never before had he been so interested or attentive.

It wasn't long before I feared that if I remained in the house I would risk becoming compromised; my stepfather's unusual amount of affection was creating a major caution in my spirit.

While no physical lines had yet been violated, I knew I couldn't stay there any longer. Without warning I had entered into crisis mode. On one level I was terrified my mother would discover the truth and make me return to Indiana, yet I instinctively knew she was the one person who would know exactly what to do. But I just couldn't bring myself to tell her.

I bartered with myself for days before I decided I couldn't live with the dread that accompanied the thought of moving back to Indiana again. So in hopes of maintaining a normal façade, I started creating excuses for spending the night at friends' houses. I'm not sure I ever truly considered what I was actually trying to accomplish or how long I thought I could pull it off; my only focus was the urgency of my situation and the need for an immediate solution. I knew I didn't want to live in Indiana but equally knew I couldn't stay in my house any longer.

I planned my escapes by pleading to friends who in turn would take me in for two or three days at a time; all the while I would fabricate reasons for my lengthened stays to my stepfather. Then when I wore out my welcome in one place, I would transfer to another friend's home or find refuge in babysitting for my cousin in a neighboring city, only to find myself having to wrestle her awake each morning—which led to consistent late arrivals to school, mounting detentions and falling grades.

After weeks of deceit my resolve weakened and the pressure became inescapable. Uncertain as to where I would stay on any given night, I began to concede the battle and just stay with my cousin, knowing it was a guaranteed "tardy" pass to class. I was growing increasingly aware that my options were thinning and my grades were suffering. All I could focus on was the constant desire to return to the normalcy of family life, which no longer existed.

I began to question whether I would have moved back had I known things would look like this—my mother gone and my life in unexpected upheaval. *At any point you can go back to Indiana,* I told myself. But I knew it wouldn't be that simple; the reality was I felt trapped—ensnared by the comfort and security I had found in familiarity and friends. My options tormented me as I walked down the hallway, oblivious to the muffled sounds of instruction that seeped through the closed wooden doors of the classrooms.

I fought to collect my thoughts as I braced myself for the class disruption I was about to cause. I stood at the door… stuck… trying to gulp in some air as I forced myself to turn the tarnished knob. My mind screamed, *Stay in the hallway ... explore your options*! but instead I silenced each individual thought and willed my feet to enter the class late for the umpteenth time.

I knew the worst part about walking into class late is that moment when every person's head turns in synchronized fashion and all eyes get fixed on the one thing that has disrupted the moment: me. It's a source of shame that enveloped me every time. And though I fought to keep myself anonymous, my efforts turned futile when Mrs. Campbell promptly ordered me right back out into the hallway.

With her hands on her hips and the sound of her toe tapping the ceramic floor echoing through the hallway, she began by reprimanding me about my "obvious level of irresponsibility." I stood at first with my eyes down, watching the pointed toe of her shoe make contact with the floor while I, with sheer determination, willed myself to not cry under her scrutiny. But when she said, "Kelly, you come from a better family than this. Exactly what do you think your sisters would say if they knew about your behavior?" my composure waned and I felt the process of self-combustion begin.

I smirked and thought about the irony of her statement. *If my sisters knew?* I sarcastically repeated to myself. I wanted to scream, "I WISH THEY DID! I WISH THEY DID KNOW!" but instead tried to focus my energy toward fighting the losing battle of my composure. My throat started to ache from restraint until the torrent of confusion and fear that had been building over the past weeks came flooding out. I gasped for breath and tried to explain about my stepfather and finding places to stay and begging my cousin every morning to get out of bed so I wouldn't be late. I wept for my circumstances and because I missed my mother, and for the pressure caused by trying to live an adult life when I was still just a kid. I wept because my sisters didn't know and for the fact that no one knew, and I wept because I was sad. And for the first time in months, I felt like somebody cared enough to notice.

Mrs. Campbell was struck silent and gently responded with open arms as I felt the emotional weight I had been carrying slowly shift from my shoulders to hers. I exhaled and cherished the feeling that came with somebody finally knowing the truth. She stood there a long time with me that day and comforted me in a way that will always remain a benchmark moment in my life. For I have come to understand that in the middle of that hallway, Mrs. Campbell loved the unlovable—despite appearance and despite what it may have cost her, she loved *me*.

I had no idea how much of a domino effect my telling Mrs. Campbell would have in my life. The truth is my "dilemma" went all the way up the chain of command, ending with my mother's impromptu visit to Ohio. It's funny how my worst fear really wasn't my stepfather or his possible actions; my biggest fear was rooted in having to move back to Indiana. So when my mother spoke at length about why I needed to return with her, I pleaded to stay, explaining, "I hated Indiana when I was there and I'm already half way through my junior year. Besides, I just received the lead in the school play." My pleading turned to begging: "Mom, I can't leave again! That would be the third major move in less than a year. Please, please let me stay."

This time the decision to stay or go wasn't mine, it was my mother's. The choice was hers and although most of the signs indicated I should return to Indiana and live with her, in the end her heart was torn: a part of her wanted to extract me from the ensuing chaos of the last months yet the other part knew full well the misery that awaited me if I returned to Indiana. She, too, was trapped in her own vortex of compassion and maternal responsibility.

After a weekend of exhausting conversations, my mother returned to Indiana alone, with only her reluctance to keep her company. I, on the other hand, remained in Ohio and moved in with my eldest stepsister and her family. Amid all the turmoil of the previous week, my mother had thought to plan and iron out all the details just in case I wanted to stay. So as I lay on my "new" bed, which had been pulled out from an old couch, I stared at the ceiling recounting life's most recent events. Unable to sleep, I let my mind wonder about the irony behind my junior high days often spent babysitting for this family as my stepsister, her husband, and their gospel group sang about the love of Jesus. Even then I recognized my unspoken connection with their message. *Perhaps that's why my mother felt the freedom to entrust me to them*, I thought. *She knew I'd be safe here.*

Feeling the need to put the pieces of my life's puzzle together, I yearned to place each event, each fact, in its proper order in my mind. I rolled on my side and looked through the narrow slat of space the pulled shade didn't cover. I shuddered at the thought of moving back to Indiana and let out a sigh that carried the weight of my thankfulness. *It's kind of bittersweet*, I thought. While I was happy to remain in Ohio, I missed the familiar routine my own family represented; I longed for my own sisters and brothers.

I scooted down further beneath the blankets, almost as if to establish my newfound place in life, and thought about the fear that motivated me the past few weeks. "It's safe here," I whispered as my body started to release the tension that all the uncertainty had caused. I felt my eyes grow heavy. I smiled at the thought of my friends and looked forward to a more normal routine. Seconds passed, and with one final glance out the window I vowed to make the adjustment to my new surroundings and to settle in to someone else's routine—even if it was without my mother.

CHAPTER THREE

Seasonal Changes

THE TWOFOLD EXCITEMENT of remaining in Ohio and feeling secure helped carry me through those initial days and weeks of living with my stepsister and her family. Kind beyond measure, they did all they could to graph me into their five member community. Yet as the excitement of those first days began to ebb, so did the surety of the decision. It wasn't long before the familiar sense of being misplaced returned and I once again found myself seeking refuge in the same way I always had: in the confines of the friends I had come to rely on so heavily in the last few months.

There was an indescribable comfort I received in the familiarity of my friends and their companionship. They were the one constant thing I could hold onto in the midst of so much change. However, what I didn't understand was that I was gradually losing my sense of definition. Although my mother had placed clear boundary lines around me, time was beginning to teach me that without her physical presence, fear of her discipline waned. And independence and rebellion slowly grew in fear's place as I struggled to survive in a world of growing obscurity.

With anonymity always lurking just below the surface, I began to challenge life in any way I could. For the first time, deception and alcohol became a part of my social life as my sense of order teetered on total chaos. Apathy toward my former structure threatened to consume me, and I grew blind to the inner war being waged deep within my soul. I felt as if two separate entities coexisted within me.

Deep inside was the innocent young girl who could identify with the nice Christian family I now lived with and who, on a Sunday afternoon when she was far away from all of the turmoil of the past six months, could quietly draw in the deepest of breaths and savor the stillness of the moments. And although I didn't fully understand why I was at peace when I was with their family, I somehow knew they provided for the truer part of me—the part that felt most genuine and real.

The other half of me was the embattled part: the hurt, angry and confused 16-year-old intensely struggling to find some sense of continuity in a world that had waged war against her understanding of innocence and truth. I felt tossed and strewn about, and all I did know was that in the midst of so much void and confusion I was losing my navigational points, which caused my previous boundary lines to grow increasingly obscure. Therefore, whatever my friends wanted to do ultimately became acceptable to me because joining in served two purposes: first, I was one of them so long as I went along—certain they wouldn't leave me—and that filled my insatiable need for acceptance. Secondly, the effect of alcohol numbed the constant pain that continually pierced my soul, ushering me from the place of following my friends to the role of now leading them.

Yet something about that particular role made me overtly uncomfortable, and the only thing that eased the discomfort was the unexpected rescues by representatives of my former life who tried to save me from becoming someone they didn't believe I was created to be. I figured they must have been given eyes to see something I had been blinded to, and eventually my perspective began to change as I adapted to my new family's routine and discovered that somehow over the past few months I had ceased feeling like a foreigner being required to live without her mother. Somehow I had become part of this nuclear family and their entire way of life, including their faith.

I remember sitting on their stairs content to just listen to their gospel group as they practiced singing about the love of Jesus and feeling His peace wash over me. It was in His presence, during those late days of spring, where the war within my soul began to ebb and I first began to genuinely experience love in its truest form—in the personhood of Jesus. He alone brought my defenses down and allowed me to come out from behind my recently created self-made fortress. Those are the days that still linger in my soul, sweet for their memory. But they were few, for just about the time I began to relax and actually let Him in, summer neared—and with it the requirement to return to Indiana.

The thought of leaving Ohio over the summer break

between my junior and senior year was less than appealing. I remembered all too well last summer and how long the days seemed. There was nothing in me that wanted a replay of that summer's isolation and loneliness, yet I wanted to spend the time with my mother. Feeling trapped again by my circumstance, I silently questioned the "whys'" that governed my situation and yearned for things to be different. But the reality was they weren't.

So the weekend after school let out I packed a summer's worth of things and headed six hours southwest on a Greyhound bus.

CHAPTER FOUR

Chance Encounters

As anticipated, that summer in Indiana was fairly uneventful though not nearly as lonely as I had feared. Spending the time with my mother was like a salve to my soul. But by the time August drew to a close, I could barely contain my excitement. The thought of returning to Ohio made my heart pound; I couldn't wait to go *home* and sleep in my own bed, and live among my own countrymen who understood how to do life together as fellow sojourners in a hostile world.

I relished in the thought that this time my return to Ohio wouldn't be during a frenzy-filled weekend. This time I was returning with a car of my own and a newfound independence that would launch me into my senior year. I started the drive back understanding that home was no longer truly defined by where my mother was, which made me incredibly sad and confused, for if I didn't belong with her then where did I really belong?

Thoughts of being 17 and a senior in high school kept me company for the first few hours of the drive. Content to travel in relative silence, I kept my eyes glued to the passing white dashes on the highway as I reflected on how different I was from the wide eyed girl who sat in the passenger seat of the rented U-Haul truck just one year ago. *Has it been that long already?* I asked myself, surprised by how fast time had gone. It seemed like yesterday when I was the frightened young girl returning to her childhood home, unsure of exactly what life would look like without my mother's daily presence. Oblivious to the hardened exterior that now shielded my vulnerabilities and made me resistant to instruction, I dismissed the anguish of the past year's circumstances and activities and smiled at the thought that in less than a year, I had actually learned how to manage without her. I didn't understand that in the midst of slowly finding my own way in a newly defined world, my mother had all but lost her voice to effectively speak into my life. All I knew was that my *place* with my friends was secure, and my home life, while different, was stable.

Lifting my eyes from the lines on the highway to my mother's car ahead of me, I watched as my sister's arms flailed in the front seat animating what must have been a lively conversation with my mother. I grew instantly aware that while I was at peace with returning to Ohio, it didn't come without a cost. I thought about the overwhelming loneliness and responsibility I felt that day in the hallway with Mrs. Campbell, and knew that living in Ohio forbade the natural camaraderie I was witnessing in my mother's car. While I desperately wanted to share life's moments with her, the reality was that despite all the turmoil of the past year, I had learned how to survive without her.

For the next few hours I let my mind travel down memory lane, reflecting on what living in Ohio used to be like when my family all lived together and the house overflowed with laughter. Then, like a light switch, my mind flipped to the last days of living with my mother and the awkward silence that filled the rooms and hallways as I witnessed the final demise of her relationship with my stepfather. Retracing those steps kept me company until I mindlessly followed my mother's lead up my cousin's gravel driveway. I wasn't half-way up the drive before I heard the escape of a tentative exhale, and I smirked at the thought of the countless times my cousin's car had sped the other way in hopes of getting me to school on time. I leaned forward as I pulled the key from the ignition, listening as the purr of the engine slowly sputtered to silence. With stillness all around, I let myself go back to the chaos of that season, then closed my eyes and offered up a silent thank you that it was all over.

I leaned back hesitant to interrupt the silent moment of peace when my mother's waving arm somehow escorted me back to reality. I started collecting my things and shifted my focus to the morning's priority of getting a job. I knew the simplicity of my plan: apply at the store where one of my older brothers had been fairly successful and use his credentials to help open the door. It seemed like an obvious, logical and innocent approach toward a necessary goal.

The following morning my mother and I planned out the day as she searched for a parking space. "Now this isn't the only place you should apply, Kelly, but you can start here," she advised.

"I know Mom, I know," I said as I exhaled, wondering if she knew she was stating the obvious. It wasn't until we rounded the corner and entered the shoe store that my mother seemed to fade into the distance as I asked to speak to the manager. I'm not sure who I expected, perhaps your stereotypical gray haired, pot bellied shoe store manager type, but I certainly wasn't prepared to meet a youthful, charismatic manager whose personality seemed to have no bounds. Without warning he was everywhere, yet possessed the alluring ability to somehow make me feel as if I was all that mattered…and I found myself completely mesmerized. Immediately smitten with his charm and good looks, I mindlessly bantered with him, forgetting all about why I had actually come to see him in the first place. Too busy savoring his attention, it wasn't until I heard the familiar sound of my mother clearing her throat that I rediscovered my focus. I glanced over at her with a silent "Okay, okay" look, only to discover that when I redirected my gaze back at him, his spell had been broken. He became complete business, and I, disappointed and helpless to recapture the moment, recognized it was time to leave with an application in my hand and a stark impression etched on my soul.

My mother and I walked down the mall corridor in silence, my mind replaying every word spoken, every magical moment of the past few minutes. I was enamored, adrift in my own reflection of our brief and sudden encounter. I lost myself in the pleasure that came from being noticed until I heard the "Ahem" of my mother's cleared throat again. As if forced to welcome an unexpected intruder into my thoughts, I stopped, let my shoulders sag, and then asked in frustration, "WHAT, Mom?"

She quickly grabbed my hand, pulled me toward the side of the corridor, and locked her eyes on mine as if she had radar and her target was in sight. Then, without hesitation and with an authority I had seldom seen her display, she commanded, "Kelly, you need to stay away from him. I do not like him and I don't want to see you hurt."

I stood just looking at her, although everything in me wanted to scream out, "I've got this!" I knew better than to verbalize my thoughts. So instead I bit my tongue and internally dismissed her warning. *What does she know?* flashed through my mind then, and just as quickly a smile emerged. I knew not to argue so instead I quickly nodded my head at her as if I was in silent agreement—fully aware that although my ears had heard her words, my heart was far from listening.

CHAPTER FiVE

Seeds of Deception

W ITH FALL WELL underway, school was in session and life became consumed with last time moments and other senior activities. Without much effort I recognized that deep in my soul I had become more settled than I had in a long time. There was a light-heartedness to my step that I had not experienced since long before my original move to Indianapolis, and I now had the freedom to seriously pursue all that interested me, including researching theatre schools in New York City. I had been waiting for this season of my life since I began high school, and although the reality of my aspirations possibly coming to pass was just months away, I could feel it as intimately as if I had already accomplished it.

I cherished every opportunity I had to step on stage because only there did I experience a comfort and confidence that eluded me in all other settings. When I was on stage I understood that it wasn't *me* people had to accept; rather, my sole responsibility was to get the audience to accept the character I would become. Therefore, the inner part of me, the one that lay beneath the newly developed hardened exterior, was protected and intact, and all the emotions I had bottled up could be poured into a particular character without ever making the inner part of me vulnerable. The character I would portray became the outlet and would inevitably become an intricate part of who I was, as if there was a mystical merge of emotions between the concrete and the abstract that occurred when I was on stage. Yet in that absorption there was little risk to me because no one, not even me at times, was able to distinguish between my story and the character's. For me, role playing was the impetus behind my initial understanding of what Shakespeare meant when he wrote,

"All the world's a stage,
And all the men and women merely players;
They have their exits and their entrances;
And one man in his time plays many parts."

I had discovered an entirely different existence on the stage, one that freed me from the invisible chains that linked my soul to its insecurities. The only thing I didn't recognize was that the release the stage brought me only lasted as long as the performance. For after the lights were down and the make-up was off, I once again existed as myself without a fictional character to deflect anyone's personal rejection.

It was during that fall production when I was summoned to the phone one afternoon by my stepsister who was frantically mouthing, "I think it's him! I think it's him!" over and over.

Taking a deep breath, I closed my eyes and willed my voice to stay as professional as a 17-year-old knew how, then said, "Hello?"

Fully expecting to set a time to come in for an interview, I was struck speechless when his request was for a date. As if time had somehow warped, I felt just as I had that Saturday morning when I was standing in the middle of the store, and once again I found myself fumbling underneath the affirmation his attention and tenacity brought me. Fighting to maintain composure, I silently waved my hands in an effort to get my stepsister's attention and, covering the mouthpiece, whisper-shouted to her, "He's asking me out! What do I do?"

Her nose wrinkled in confusion then her eyes grew larger as she resolutely shook her head NO and whispered back, "You need that job. Tell him thank you, but no." I felt my shoulders sink in disappointment, then looked at her one more time, scouring for a crack in her armor. I closed my eyes and tried to stir up the resolve to decline his offer, listening as he mentioned something about dinner and a movie, and although I was reluctant to interrupt I heard myself say, "I'm sorry." Then as politely as I could, I thanked him but declined his offer, all the while hoping he would call me for an interview.

When his assistant manager called a few days later, the idea that professional lines had already been violated never truly crossed my mind—nor did the concept that perhaps my mother's warning, in the end, did have some merit. Therefore it never dawned on me to question why he was the one who trained me or why every time I was scheduled to work, it was with him. Equally, I never grew suspicious about no one ever working with us; those facts weren't something my eyes chose to see. From my perspective whatever pleasure that came from working with him was harmless; he simply made me laugh. And even though I could acknowledge that our playfulness was increasing, it was all still innocent to me—I viewed it as simple fun. Besides, the explanation of his marital status was always lingering in the back of my mind, and I couldn't seem to dismiss the idea that while he was separated from his wife and currently living with two male roommates, he was still married. So while my attraction to him was growing increasingly difficult to ignore, something about his situation felt far beyond my 17-year-old scope of life.

For the first few months I maintained my perspective and kept him at bay. However, just as I had learned over time how to survive without my mother, I would also come to learn that deception doesn't just arbitrarily happen; most often it's a process. And in that process, there is a luring that occurs that defies all logical explanation. Certainly my mother's warning resurfaced time to time, and even my guardians were faithful to voice their concerns about my increasing involvement with him. But both would immediately grow dim in light of how he made me feel. His daily attention and concern for me or how my day had gone was too difficult to resist. And although I tried to do the noble thing and refuse to date him because he was married, my sense of nobility began to dissolve almost as quickly as the warnings.

Shadows of truth fought to keep the gates of resistance closed, but they were little match for the one thing that prevailed as constant in my soul: the driving need to be accepted. That need slowly, and oftentimes daily, began to get satisfied in the face of his unwavering attention and affirmation. Therefore, despite all apprehensions and admonitions, what began as innocent and fun grew into an emotional fix for a security starved junkie. His attention, his mere presence began to draw me like a magnetic force. And regardless of how I tried to say no or resist his effect, I found myself losing my will to stay away from him. Little by little my resolve began to buckle and all the rational reasons why I should say no ceased to matter. I knew one thing during those days: he was *there* and for the first time in what felt like a long time, I had a sense of belonging when I was with him. Everything else I could justify my way around.

CHAPTER SIX

Taking Root

ONCE THE DECISION to venture into a dating relationship with him was made, it didn't take long before spending time with him became my sole focus. If I wasn't at school and we weren't working, we were doing other things together. Though the relationship was entirely platonic, the magnetic force drawing us together emotionally was beginning to do its work physically as well.

Certainly there were times when physical subtleties would present themselves, but I typically put them under the same category as our flirting. The resisted kiss …the passing glance … merely innocent byproducts of two people who were growing to care for one another. Never did I plan for nor expect things to go any further; I hadn't with my other boyfriends and I didn't with him. I just thoroughly enjoyed our time together, and with each passing day, I grew more secure and confident in his presence. In my simple teenage mind our relationship made complete sense because he was *there*. He was there every day asking all the right questions and paying the right kind of attention to me, so he was the one I began seeking reassurance from. It became just a matter of time before he, unbeknownst to either of us, took the place my mother had once played in my life. He became my sole counselor, my confidant, and my "go to" person.

Our increased time together seemed to just naturally reflect my growing dependency on him; the two things somehow became inseparable. By mid-December I was hooked, and despite all warnings, reprimands and attempted blockades I knew one thing: There was *nothing* and *no one* that would keep me from him. In my mind, I had already given up too much and believed firmly that because I had survived the last 18 months of chaos and upheaval, I had earned the right to voice my opinion and ultimately to demand the freedom to make my own decision.

Shortly thereafter, realizing that logistically speaking there was little she could do to corral my newfound independence, my mother respectfully attempted to establish boundary lines during a three way meeting. She demanded from him that I be honored physically, to which he seemingly agreed while I sat, a silent observer in the meeting, my body refusing to sit still due to the awkwardness that hung like a thick cloud over the room. I sat, my fingers finding purpose in rolling my paper napkin back and forth, and watched my mother from across the table. I wondered if this was difficult for her, and for one of the first times in my life, was overwhelmed by the vast expanse my father's absence had caused—not only for me but for her as well. *She shouldn't have to do this,* I thought. Then the internal questions followed... *Shouldn't he be here?... If Dad was here...* But there were no answers so the questions stagnantly lingered in my mind, unspoken and unresolved.

Without the presence of my father, I found the meeting pointless and desperately wanted it to end. Instead I had to watch and listen as two of my favorite people battled out their individual perspectives on what time with me should look like. It was clear she despised him, and the more I rose to his defense, the deeper her disdain became. I felt like I was in the battle of my life for I had grown to completely adore him but knew my mother's approval would never be forthcoming. So I was back right where everything began. I felt just like I did when I had to choose between living with my mom and moving back to Ohio. Only this time, I had to choose between him and my mother's approval. I knew she would never disown or forsake me; it was a different type of choice. This was a choice of fellowship. Who would I choose to share my life with, my daily circumstances? Who would I allow to influence me? I knew sitting at that table that being in relationship with him was not something I would be able to openly share with her, and therein lay the choice, which was really no choice at all. He was there in all the ways I needed him and she wasn't, and that was the single largest determining factor to all of my decisions—both now and any that may loom in the future.

CHAPTER SEVEN
Thorns and Thistles

FROM AN OUTSIDER'S perspective I was clearly in over my head, but from my vantage point everything felt like it was under control. With our relationship fairly out in the open, I was free to pursue what I believed was normal with regards to dating. I obeyed curfews and remained compliant with the preset boundary lines my mother had put in place and reiterated with my guardians. In my world, all appeared innocent and intact. Though fully enthralled with our time together, I was maintaining the physical lines fairly well. At my core I believed in the concept of abstinence, and because I had never really been confronted with a viable opportunity, it was fairly easy to articulate my convictions that waiting until marriage was my goal. It wasn't until I was emotionally rocked through my current relationship that I began to discover how difficult a commitment it would be to keep.

The definitive lines that had once been indelibly drawn were slowly becoming less tangible, and with each weakening "no" the steps toward "yes" became easier to take. Just as deception often comes through process, so does compromise. It was quickly becoming apparent to me that after evenings which would end with my barely escaping a full "yes," I would wake up the next morning thanking God that I still had my virginity. While these mornings seemed to be growing in frequency, I failed to recognize them or categorize them as another form of warning. Despite my apparent gratitude toward my purity, I slowly became convinced that pushing on the boundary lines was the primary indicator of just how emotionally attached I was becoming to him.

By the time I fully surrendered myself to him, responsible or safe sex was the furthest thing from my mind. I remember telling him I didn't want to get pregnant, and his response was simply, "You won't. Trust me."

It's funny how a young woman's mind works; emotionally I was completely his, and therefore, his words were like an arrow that had been shot straight at the bull's eye. Trusting him was the one thing I was capable of, for I had already bared the deepest part of my soul with him. Why shouldn't I trust him? He clearly was experienced, and I, who had no experience, was completely naïve and vulnerable to my dependency on him. So, at that moment, I chose to believe what he said and with a silent "yes," allowed my physical consent to be the natural manifestation of where my heart had already gone.

The morning after was somehow different from previous mornings when I used to wake up emitting a sigh of relief. Mysteriously enough, I felt bonded to him in an indescribable way, and while the thought of what we had shared made it difficult for me to look right at him, I knew my actions had somehow sealed the deal. They took my heart to a whole new level of emotion with him, and somewhere along the way I had lost the ability to identify who I was apart from him. From that point forward, who I was when I was with him was all that truly mattered. So while I went through the motions of submitting college applications, for the most part they were mindless acts of conformity. The only one I truly cared about was the interview with the Admissions Department of the American Academy of Dramatic Arts (AADA) that I had been aggressively pursuing.

I often wondered during that time if things could have been any better, because it seemed as if the new year was taking perfect shape. I treasured the feeling of having my life exactly as I wanted it. Gone were last year's moments of uncertainty and fear, and my former companion named Silence was no longer my best friend. I believed I had truly turned the corner and the worst was far behind me for I was halfway through my senior year and more content than I remembered being in a long time.

~~~~~

He began acting oddly toward the end of January and I was taken completely off guard. Certainly I had placed few demands on him due to my own hectic schedule, but during the past few days at work I noticed he had grown aloof and was arguably avoiding me. Of course, my own internal mechanisms began to spin their wheels as I personalized his behavior. The old thoughts that had tormented me most of my life came in soft whispers but grew louder with each odd encounter. *What did you do now? ... See, he doesn't really like you ... you must have done something...*

Deathlike fear began to grip my soul, for if my insecurities proved to be true then massive guilt would consume me. *How would I ever reconcile being intimate with a man who obviously had no real feelings for me?* I questioned. *Maybe Mom was right,* I thought as the internal battles took turns erupting. I walked around the store, uncertainty following me wherever I went. Because I had made him my sole source of life and affirmation, I began to cling to him with an intensity comprised of sheer desperation and survival.

I asked. I prodded. And to my dismay, I begged until he finally looked at me toward the end of January, angry and frustrated, and hollered, "My wife's pregnant and frankly, Kelly, I'm afraid you are, too."

Reality has a strange way of targeting its victims. At that moment the shock of all that his statement entailed felt like something had stuck its clawlike hand down my throat, stretched its long fingers across my lungs and pulled the air back out of my esophagus, leaving it to hang somewhere in the room. I couldn't think, let alone breathe.

Time was immeasurable. It couldn't have been long before I responded with a quick denial in a measly effort to stabilize my crashing dream world, as if refusing to accept the truth could really keep out the facts that were now threatening my newly secured utopia. What I was denying more fiercely, his pregnant wife or my possible pregnant status, I still don't know. I just knew neither fit into my plan.

Air slowly found its way back into my body as logic began

to win out over emotion. I would have to deal with the facts first and my own possibility second. Despite my own apparent belief that I had matured to a state of adult independence, I admittedly approached his confession with a high school mentality. I began rationalizing his "unfaithfulness" as a one-time thing, otherwise why would he have such obvious remorse over his wife's condition? And since she was already three months pregnant, his encounter with her preceded any serious relational development with me, so of course his remorse was genuine. These two "facts" alone were enough for me to emotionally reestablish myself and slowly begin to accept this new unexpected complication. The unspoken pressure of potentially having two women pregnant at the same time never entered my mind as a possible cause for his emotional distress; the only thing I saw was a person who wanted me as much as I wanted him to want to be there. Everything else seemed secondary at that moment.

Throughout the following week I checked the mail daily for news from the AADA, anticipating possible interview dates. All the while his secondary statement of my possible pregnancy lingered in the back of my mind. I was never one to track my cycles, so I had no idea if I was early, late or on time and, for the moment, that was enough to keep my nerves at bay.

In the meantime, there was little anyone could do to keep us away from one another and word had slowly gotten back to my mother, who began to press me on how far I had gone with him sexually. Fully aware of my potential conflict, I admitted that I had been with him and she immediately reminded me of the risks involved with such a decision. She then promptly scheduled a doctor's appointment for me. I had no plans on telling her what his biggest fear was at the moment; in my mind she didn't need any more fuel for her fire, so I just played along.

It was mid-week when the AADA letter came in the mail inviting me to New York City for an interview. I was elated, rushing to the phone wanting him to be the first person I told. He briefly shared my excitement, then quickly followed up with "Have you gone to the doctor yet?" Frustrated with the fact that that thought always had to be the spoken or unspoken killjoy, I curtly explained it was the next day and I would be sure to let him know how it went, then abruptly hung up.

The following school day dragged on as the doctor's appointment loomed over me. It had been just over a week since the announcement about his wife's pregnancy had been made, followed by his unexpected suspicion. Ten long days of not knowing had somehow passed, taking me to the point of desperately wanting some firm answers—regardless of their outcome.

That same false bravado accompanied me as I pulled into the doctor's parking lot. I felt completely at odds with myself and incredibly uncomfortable. He had been our family doctor for as long as I could remember, and having to face him under these circumstances made the familiar reminiscent feeling of uncertainty begin to rear its head. Shame greeted me as I checked in for the appointment, then enveloped me as I answered the nurse's prodding questions. I wasn't prepared for my decisions to be put on display, and for the first time since late December I became overtly conscious of my actions. I began to question their validity, rendering me speechless and unable to lift my gaze in the examination room.

After the exam I sat up and watched as he scribbled something on my chart, desperately wanting to know what it said but too afraid to ask. In the entire ten minute encounter, neither he nor the nurse spoke a word to me. He just silently wrote two scripts and sent me on my way; I never questioned why there were two.

CHAPTER EIGHT

Unmitigating Circumstances

THE SAME UNCERTAINTY that had accompanied every minute of the school day seemed to greet me at the front of the store as he welcomed me with what felt like an inquisition: "What did he say? Did he say when you would start? What did he give you?"

Trying to hold his questions at bay, I just looked at him and said, "Hold on, okay?" and slowly walked back into the stock room. I was as nervous as he was, and his firestorm of questions wasn't helping alleviate the stress level in either of us. I took a deep breath, turned to look at him and with the same mustered up courage that led me into the doctor's office, tried to calmly reassure him. "He gave me a script for birth control and said I was fine. I should start any day." Then I asked him, "Weren't you the one that said I wouldn't get pregnant? What are you so worried about? Perhaps this is your turn to trust that

49

everything will be okay."

Shortly after our initial "heart to heart," he called me to the store phone and told me my mother was on the line, which struck me incredibly odd. I looked at him as if to ask if she had said anything but he just shrugged his shoulders in a bewildered manner and walked back out on the floor. I turned to pick up the receiver and for the third time that afternoon, took a deep inhale and quietly said, "Hello?"

It's funny how the sound of one's voice can set the mood of an entire conversation, even if you can't see the person. I knew as soon as I heard her utter her faint hello, something was very wrong. My mother, even today, is one of the strongest women I've ever known. She is not easily thrown off guard nor is she often without a plan of action, yet her voice completely betrayed her controlled façade. She was, at best, shaken but remained undeterred in getting to the point of her call. "Kelly, what did the doctor say to you?"

I repeatedly explained that he didn't say anything to me, only that he did the exam and wrote two scripts, but he never said a word. She continued to press for information. "Kelly, do *you* know what the second script was for?"

Frustrated I responded, "Mom, I don't know. I know one was for the pill he wanted to put me on, but I couldn't read the other one."

She said, "Did you ask him?"

"No. He was weird; I just wanted to get out of there."

She was quiet for what felt like a long time, and I didn't know what to say so I just twirled the phone cord and waited for her to speak. "Kelly, I just spoke with him...he thinks you're pregnant. The second script is for a blood test he wants drawn tomorrow."

Silence invaded our conversation like an unwelcome visitor. For weeks, in the face of constant reminders that pregnancy could be a real possibility, I had been able to keep the reality at bay. I always believed it was just a thought derived from a vain imagination; it never had any real merit in my mind. I didn't feel pregnant. I wasn't sick. I was still me. My mother's repeated, "Kelly," then with more force, "KELLY," summoned me back to real time.

"Okay...okay. I'll go tomorrow," I quickly murmured, barely able to breathe. I felt void of all air, as if the wind had been knocked out of me. I heard her say something about being home tomorrow evening and that we needed to talk, but my mind had already started strategizing exactly how I was going to tell him, so I mindlessly agreed to whatever she was saying, said goodbye, then hung up.

How do I do this? I asked myself, leaning my head against the wall. A whirlwind of chaos swirled around me. His wife, my college interview, that first night with him … snippets of events flashed through my mind like snapshots. *How did this happen?* my mind scoured for an answer. This was the last thing that was supposed to occur. Air slowly refilled my lungs as I began mentally rehearsing how to tell him. Realizing there was no way around it, I decided I would just start with what I knew—the blood test.

It was easier than I originally suspected, in part because my own shock was still evident when he walked through the doorway. I wasn't quite ready for his sudden appearance so as soon as he looked at me he knew. I desperately resisted the urge to cry as I shared with him the doctor's concern, and waited for him to offer some kind of reassurance. I wanted him to reach out, to beckon me to himself so the momentum of emotion threatening to envelop me could find its release. But he didn't. So, for the second time in just minutes, I found myself stricken by Silence as I stood there unable to do anything but watch him grow increasingly angry with me, then listen as he hollered something about not needing this in his life right now.

I was already buckling from the sheer heaviness of the circumstance, and his reluctance to help bear the weight of my situation felt like a thick wet blanket that got laid on top of the news my mother had just shared with me. It felt as if my world was whirling around me and I was stuck in its vortex with no voice to shout for help and no way to save myself.

I listened to his fury erupt at me and, like clips from a silent movie, the events of the last month began rolling through my mind again. My surrender to him began the trailer, then the despair of discovering his wife's pregnancy preceded the sheer elation of the possible interview with the American Academy of Dramatic Arts. Then, like a rollercoaster, both of those events became the car carrying me on a quick ascent toward the newly discovered major climax—my own pending pregnancy.

I stood in that doorway numb and unsure of exactly how I was supposed to feel. He was screaming, my mother was devastated and I had no place to put any of it. I was overwhelmed and knew that the only place I would find comfort in the face of such unexpected turmoil was in the companionship of my faithful friend named Silence. So I did the only thing I knew to do ... I quietly turned around, gathered my belongings and, despite his demands to come back, I left the store.

CHAPTER NINE

Reaping the Harvest

I WOKE THE next morning with the same familiar feeling
that had once kept me company during the first weeks
of living without my mother—emotional isolation. I was
completely alone. Not in the literal sense, but in every other
way: emotionally, mentally and spiritually. If what the doctor
suspected was true, I knew it was just a matter of time before
the "I told you so" people would surface and compound the
stupid feeling that had already begun to take residence in my
soul. Moreover, the person that I had given and entrusted
myself to, despite all warnings, had begun to strike dents in
what was once an indestructible suit of armor.

"So, now what?" I whispered, looking at the ceiling. The
shame of my actions propelled me into deeper silence. There
was no way I could share this possibility with any of my
friends. If fear of their rejection haunted me while growing

up, what would being pregnant at 17 by a married man who had his wife pregnant at the same time do to their acceptance of me? I was stuck, frightened and without a lot of options. The only thing I could do was go to the lab, get the blood test and try to function normally in hopes that no one would notice anything was wrong.

Much like the day before, the school day dragged on as I silently willed the clock to tick faster. I tapped my foot, rapped my pencil and drummed my fingers all the way to the 3:30 p.m. bell then frantically drove to the lab. It wasn't until after the technician had drawn the blood that they informed me the results wouldn't be in until mid-week the next week. I sunk into a new overwhelming despair. "Mid-week? Really? That's at least five more days," I said. They politely apologized, explaining there was nothing more they could do.

By the time I got back to my car, my nerves had escalated into an all time high alert frenzied state. Both sides of the possibilities repeatedly tormented me... *What if I am?* followed by *What if I'm not?*... then they would start over as if someone had hit the replay button. It had been nearly two weeks since I had first started to dance this crazy dance and I just needed to know. So I decided, despite all circumstantial awkwardness, to drive to a nearby clinic and beg for a pregnancy test.

If discreet was on my radar, it ceased to exist as the tinkle of the bell announced my opening of the door. I stood in the entrance and looked at the stairs leading up to the doors of the clinic and took in the old musty smell that seemed to emit from the surrounding woodwork. I stood, frozen in time, thinking about how surreal everything felt. *Never did I plan on being the one to have to do this,* I thought. I glanced back up and counted the ten steps in front of me—ten steps would carry me from uncertainty to actually knowing. I felt my hand relax its grip on the door and began gradually inching myself upward, each step creaking beneath my weight.

When I reached the top of the stairs, I looked through the glass door and felt relief wash over me as I realized no other clients were there. When I reached to pull the door toward me, my stomach flipped and I felt the bile slowly creep up my throat. I closed my eyes and swallowed hard in hopes of forcing it back down when an immeasurably kind and reassuring woman, whose eyes comforted my nerves long before she ever answered my questions, rounded the corner to greet me.

She sat with me for a long time and listened as I shared all the sordid details of my evolving situation, all the while holding my hand or gently rubbing my back. But in the end, she apologetically informed me that without my mother's consent she couldn't test me, but she assured me she would keep me in her prayers. I looked at her and gave her a half hearted smile, hoping she would understand my silent message of gratitude. Then I reluctantly tried to accept that, despite all my best efforts toward self-discovery, I would have to wait a while longer. So, after collecting myself one final time, I quietly left to meet my mother who was en route from Indianapolis.

It didn't take long for the shame and stupidity that had been battering at my soul for the past two days to resurface as I drove and tried to prepare myself for seeing my mother in person. Gone was the false sense of protection the phone lines had once brought me; in its place were conjured up imaginary conversations and reactions, all centered on creating some line of defense for my unexplainable actions.

Unlocking the door, I remembered coming home when I was a little girl and she would send me to my room to wait for my punishment; I never knew what was worse, the waiting or the punishment. Yet here I was waiting all over again, but somehow the discipline felt so much more permanent and consequential than when I was young. I glanced at the clock and began mentally rehearsing the possible scenarios when suddenly the sound of her voice drifted through the back hallway entrance and my mental journeys immediately ceased their travel. Instantly I felt all of my mustered up resolve and collectedness of the past few days drain from my body.

I heard the mumbled hello's and strained greetings, and was immediately compelled by an overwhelming need to see her. It wasn't that I suddenly didn't care what her reaction would be … it was more that my need to know, my need for something concrete in my life drove me off the couch and around the corner. But as soon as our eyes met my will to move failed me and I was paralyzed—frozen in place, as if my shame had somehow erected an invisible barrier between us.

She didn't speak a word, but I knew through one look at me … her eyes conveyed everything she couldn't say. It wasn't anger or disgust or disappointment I saw. On the contrary, her eyes were a pure reflection of the compassion that consumed her. And then, as if she knew it was the only way to get me to move, she opened her arms as a silent way to welcome me and I immediately felt the freedom to run. So I ran. And though I ran in shame and regret, I ran and found comfort in the one person who despite her physical absence had always been there for me.

The next morning my mother provided me an early

pregnancy test and told me that whenever I was ready, she would be right there. I silently nodded in agreement, then turned toward the bathroom. If I thought fear had become a permanent fixture to my existence while I waited for my mother, waiting and watching for the formation of my future to appear on a little test strip was paralyzing. For all the times I thought knowing the truth would be better than wondering, I suddenly found myself desperately wanting those last few minutes of imaginary freedom to last forever.

In those few moments, life somehow had once again begun to feel normal. My mother was with me, and if I tried really hard I could pretend that the last year and a half had never really happened. For the first time in days, the silence that was all around seemed to bring with it a calm that lingered in the air until my thoughts would refocus and remind me exactly why we were waiting. I stared at the test, my lower lip taking the brunt of my nervous energy until slowly and without much warning the little pink circle began to emerge, declaring my pregnancy.

I'll never fully know if my mother returned to Ohio emotionally prepared for that moment or not, but when her voice broke into the silence, the wisdom it carried somehow reverberated through all of time. In a simple three minute conversation she slowly said, "Well, Kelly, it looks like you have some decisions to make," then paused to look at me. "You can have this baby and release it for adoption or you can have this baby and keep it. But realize if that's what you decide, it's yours—*you* will raise this baby. I will help you when I can, but this is your responsibility, not mine." Pausing, she quietly continued, "However, if you choose to abort this baby, you are on your own. I will not help you with that decision."

And, that was it. There was no condemnation, no shouting and no reprimands—at least not from her. She simply viewed it through the lenses that since I had made the decision to be intimate with him, it was now my decision to govern the life that had found its way in me.

Little did I know how much weight that one decision would carry ... for every one of us.

CHAPTER TEN
Moment of Truth

FOR THE FIRST time since I had started working I dreaded going into the store. Nothing in me was prepared to see him, partly because I was still reeling from the infamous pink circle that had appeared earlier that morning and I needed my own time to process. I thought about the options my mother had laid before me and how much easier the decision would be if he felt differently, but the remnants of his last tirade still echoed through my mind, painting a much harsher reality. *How do I tell him I'm pregnant when he doesn't want anything to do with it?* I asked myself. *What do I say to him when I don't even know what to tell myself?*

I fumbled around for answers but in looking back have come to realize that he must have instinctively known as soon as I walked into the store, because as soon as he saw me he immediately took his break and escorted me right back out. Keeping his hand firmly gripped on my elbow, he steered me through the mall corridors, never once saying a word, but the tension between us somehow said it all. I struggled to maintain my composure as the familiar internal voices of blame and accusation started their recital and all I could think was, *I don't need this right now.* What I really wanted was for him to look at me, to help talk me through this like he had all the other times. Instead he averted my gaze and silently marched me around as if I was a little kid who had gotten into some kind of trouble.

Seconds after he let go of my arm, we stopped and sat at a corner table in the food court and, for the first time since I entered the store, I looked at him. Every part of me ached to see the person I thought I knew, and as I searched my love of language for just the right words to tell him about this morning, he suddenly blurted out, "Kelly, you have to have an abortion. I can't have this kid."

With a force all their own, his words reached across the table and sucked all the air from my gut. I sat there speechless trying to make sense out of what he just said. I couldn't tell what was more disturbing … the sheer thought of an abortion or the fact that he, this man whom I connected with in every way, could suggest such a thing. I looked at him, stunned by his apparent lack of sensitivity, and said, "No. I can't."

"Can't or won't?" he candidly asked.

"Both," I replied, then looked down, hating the tears that were beginning to make everything blurry.

But he wasn't finished. He began formulating his persuasive argument by stating the obvious: I was only 17. I had my whole future in front of me. Then he asked me, "You still want to go to college, don't you? Isn't that what you've been working toward?" Then he paused, as if he had to reset his target before he finished with, "Have you thought about how all this affects me, considering my wife's pregnant? I can't have two more kids, Kelly."

His last question hung in the air like a cloud of stench, and my eyes burned for the rancidness it brought with it. I sat back in my chair and closed my eyes, silently begging for it to all be just a bad nightmare. But instead, the reality of my dire circumstances flashed like a neon sign in my mind and the more he continued speaking and building his case toward abortion, the more my fear began to seek its escape through his finely constructed exit sign.

I resisted his idea for as long as I could but the longer he argued his case, the more I allowed myself to consider the possibility that maybe my mother's options were a bit narrow-minded after all. *What if there was more available to me than just what she presented?* I asked myself. *If I do things his way, no one would ever have to know how stupid I had been. If he's right, my life would return to the way it was and my future would still be in front of me.*

Those thoughts lingered and replayed in my mind, bringing with them an unexpected comfort in the idea of not having to be pregnant. I felt the whirlwind of everyone knowing and giving up college begin to settle as I silently entertained all of the options made available. Desperate to find a way out of the chaos and torment that had become my life the past 48 hours, I suddenly realized that if there was any way I could roll the clock back, it would be through an abortion.

Could I? I questioned. *I want my life back ...the life I had before December*, I told myself. So, without warning, in the face of sheer desperation, what had once been a repulsive option was gradually becoming somewhat appealing. It was the one option that seemed to hold the most hope of restoring some level of sanity to what had become an incredibly insane world. "Okay," I told him, then paused knowing I wasn't ready to fully concede to his idea. "I'll think about it."

The next week passed, bringing with it a growing sensitivity to smells and an unusual attraction to saltine crackers. I spent most of my time alone trying to sort out how I felt about things while the world around me carried on normally. My internal pendulum swung from side to side as I silently deliberated my options. It wasn't until the following weekend through a conversation with my cousin that it seemed to find its resting place.

I was more candid in that conversation than I had been in any other. My mother had already confided in her about my pregnancy, so from the onset of my arrival she asked what felt like a million questions, and for the first time since hearing about his wife's pregnancy, I was completely transparent. I told her everything, from my audition letter to his wanting me to get an abortion because he didn't want two women pregnant at the same time. My need to protect his character was waning in the face of so much controversy and decision making, and I needed someone to help me process.

She listened for a long time as I unloaded all that had confronted me the past week and allowed the room to grow silent after I was finished, then just looked at me. I expected a verbal rebuke questioning how I could let this happen or probing inquiries as to why I didn't get away from him sooner. Yet she spoke neither of those. Instead, without much reaction at all, she simply offered to make an appointment with a family friend of hers who was a doctor and would "take care of everything."

This time the words didn't carry nearly as much force but yet reverberated with fierce similarity everything he had argued just a week ago: I was 17, my entire future was in front of me...he was married, she was pregnant... On and on she went, but she added one major point that he never mentioned. Simply, that where I was at in the pregnancy meant all I had was a mass of tissue; I didn't really have a baby so it wouldn't be a big deal. Then, as if on cue, she completed her case by offering once again to line up the appointment, reassuring me that no one but she and I would know and it would be over in minutes. And, most importantly, she guaranteed I would get my life back and things could return to normal.

The fear of a crisis pregnancy is indescribable unless you have experienced it. There is no doubt that American society in 1983 viewed the unplanned and/or an unwed pregnancy of a 17-year-old vastly differently than our 21st century society does. Regardless, for me, at that moment, my cooperation with shame, guilt and regret led me on a road that didn't seem to allow U-turns. Coupling my own internal strife with the persuasive arguments being made to abort, I felt like I was standing on the edge of a cliff waiting to jump and all I lacked was the courage to bend my knees and power myself off. I knew I was being swayed—in part because of my own fear regarding what my new life would require, the other part just seemed logical.

I left my cousin's house that evening with still no one to really talk to, which required me to ponder the decision completely alone. The case had been made; now all I had to do was settle it in my own heart. Secretly, I prayed that I would miscarry or that something would happen to restore my life to its previous setting. Yet nothing ever did.

Days passed and I longed to find outside support for a decision I dared to take comfort in. I already knew where my mother stood so I couldn't talk with her about it, but mid-week my sister called to ask me how I was doing and where I was in my decision making process. Like a floodgate bulging to be let open, I began to share my heart, my fears and my pending decision. I repeated, like a parrot, both persuasive conversations and found myself reciting points I wasn't even sure I believed. What I did believe in was the thought of normalcy, not abortion. But I argued. I argued relentlessly—I wanted my life back and if this was the only way I could have it then I didn't understand what the big deal was. After all, it was just a mass of tissue, right?

It's funny how the memory of a conversation can remain with you, but the specifics of that conversation diminish. I can still see myself on the phone with her in my guardians' bedroom. I know exactly what I was wearing and I remember it was snowing. I also know that in the midst of fighting for survival as I knew it, my sister stood for life. I know that while she disapproved of what I had done, she encouraged me with grace to face what lay ahead and she spoke profound truth into a whirlwind of deceit. Her words, while not specifically recounted on paper, cast a major light into a world of darkness and she helped strengthen me to choose life that day, regardless of its cost.

It was late that night in the midst of all that had occurred over the past few weeks when my spirit kept me awake and my eyes refused to close. Like a baby deer unsure of its first steps, my initial decision to not have an abortion seemed easier to make when my sister was on the phone. But the reality of 400-plus miles of separation began to consume me and I was once again left alone to face my circumstances. With Silence as my only faithful companion, I quietly crawled out of bed, bundled up and drove to the one place I knew solace would find me.

As I drove my '76 red Chevy Nova into the parking lot, random snowflakes gently fell in front of my headlights reminding me that not all was in upheaval. Even in their gentle descent, peace was found. Getting out of the car, silence surrounded me as I quietly shut the car door; it was late, far too late for a 17-year-old girl to be out trying to find her way in life. The only other participants who came out to welcome me in my search were the moon and the snowflakes that began to caress the newly built altar. I began my cautious approach toward the shrine built to Mary, the mother of Jesus, knowing full well it wasn't her I was looking for; I needed Him.

It was a moment that has forever stopped in time for me— the full reality of my situation compelled me to my knees and I cried out with everything I had, *Please, Lord, I don't know if I can do this. I am so frightened.* Remorse poured from my soul and sorrow consumed me. I begged, pleaded and cajoled with the Lord that if there was any other way to please release me. When there were no more words, tears spoke for me and so I wept. I wept for all that I had given up and all that I had surrendered, and I again asked the Lord, *If Lord...if there is any way, would You? I don't want to do this.*

Time was infinite until the tears began to subside. Silence

65

was the sole connection between the girl on the kneeling bench and her God when suddenly He very gently spoke, *"Kelly, I will work all things together for your good. Even this."*

And almost instantly, I somehow knew that in the midst of all that I had done, with one spoken word a tangible peace had invaded the midst of my storm. I remained still, eyes closed, afraid of shattering the moment; instead, I tried to breathe it in and allow the reality of having this baby sink into my soul. Time was immeasurable, and while I can't say fear was completely absent, I can say it was no longer the driving force behind my decision. His reassurance took its place, and ultimately would gradually become the bedrock of my soul and the first layer of an indestructible foundation.

CHAPTER ELEVEN

Securing the Foundation

MAKING THE DECISION to choose life was like jumping the first of many hurdles that stood in front of me. The second was the responsibility of telling certain people who needed to hear the news from me. At the top of the list were the people I lived with who still had no idea of the events of the past week, so I had some understanding that my news would come as a bit of a shock—which made breaking the news even more challenging.

Second to my fear of sharing my news was the embarrassment I believed my actions would cause them since Bob was not only a teacher at my high school but a beloved pastor as well. The last thing I wanted was for my current single-and-pregnant-by-a-married-man-whose-wife-was-also-pregnant status to mark Bob's reputation like a scarlet letter. I braced myself for their disapproval and discipline, and assumed my news would require me to move back to Indiana once and for all. But arguably at this point, although it wasn't what I wanted, it certainly wasn't the most difficult thing I would have to face.

It took some time for me to drum up enough courage to admit what still felt like an inconceivable thing. It wasn't until one evening after play practice while I warmed up dinner and talked with both of them about the day that I tried to maneuver the conversation toward the truth. Initially, we spoke of school and tests and how I was doing, which suddenly felt like the natural segue into my news. So during the first lull in the conversation I quickly said, "Hey, I need to tell you both something, but first please know I'm really... really sorry."

While those words themselves didn't carry an enormous amount of information, the tone and pace of their utterance did, filling the room with expectancy, concern and silence, as if anything else spoken would break my momentum. I sat straight up and took turns looking at both of them before I said, "I took a test over the weekend ...a pregnancy test. It came out positive." I looked down, afraid to see their reaction.

Seconds passed by, and while there's not much that I remember about that moment, the image of Bob leaning on the counter with a dishtowel in his hand, processing my news in what felt like a millisecond, will always remain with me. I waited for the rebuke but then suddenly, without any hesitation, he just looked at me, shrugged his shoulders and simply said, "Well, at least you passed a test," then walked over and put his arms around me.

I've often reflected on his response, and over time have realized that it will most likely always remain with me for it has become a watershed moment in my life. Bob's reaction was my first tangible encounter to God's infinite grace. Without any further explanation I understood that while Bob didn't condone my actions, he never condemned me for them. Instead, these two people, the two whom I had grown up with and babysat their children as they spread the gospel, promised to wholeheartedly support my decision for life and allowed me to remain with them regardless of whatever personal shame or embarrassment my actions may bring them. They, like Mrs. Campbell, chose to love the unlovable and taught me that because God cannot and will not despise a broken and contrite heart, they wouldn't either.

The following Saturday, I set out to see two of my favorite people outside of my immediate family—my aunt and uncle on my father's side and, according to Catholic tradition, my godparents. Staunch in their faith and unwavering in their love for me, they faithfully tried to fill the massive vacancy my father's death had created.

As I drove the twenty minutes across town, I reminisced about when my aunt and uncle would take my siblings and me camping for long weekends even though their camper was overflowing with their own seven children. The sweet memories made me smile and I thought about how they symbolized what a functional family really looked like. I had grown to feel deeply accountable to them over the years and I knew this was not going to be an easy conversation.

Dreariness hung in the air as I walked up the familiar steps to their back door. I took a deep breath and wondered if, on some level, this is what it would feel like to tell my father and face his disappointment. My heart raced, sending its beat reverberating in my ears as I opened the back door. My uncle, seated in *his* chair with his faithful coffee cup and newspaper before him, looked up, smiled and greeted me with, "Well, look who's here."

I couldn't help but smile at him and walked over, kissed him on his cheek, and asked where my aunt was. Once she joined us, the conversation flowed as usual. We spoke of my cousins and siblings and how everyone was doing, etc. I remember being struck by how unexpectedly difficult this felt for I knew my news would break their hearts. I took a hard swallow and began to feel grief spread across my chest because, for the first time, I realized that my actions, the ones I used to feel were so personal, were inevitably going to cause other people so much pain.

I fidgeted in the face of such a realization and tried to pretend that I didn't really need to tell them. I hesitated and avoided their eye contact as I tried to find the most opportune time to deliver the most inopportune news. When my aunt finally asked me, "So, what brings you all the way over here?" I simply replied that I just wanted to see them, but she didn't believe me. So after a few seconds I said, "I need to share something with you that isn't easy to say and won't be easy to hear," and then I told them.

Their collective anger was the first to manifest, but it wasn't directed at me. My stoic aunt simply said, "Oh, Kelly." But my uncle, the one who made me smile every time I thought of him—the one whose approval always mattered—looked at me and sternly stated, "You know, Kelly, if your father was here he would kill him."

My initial reaction wanted to find comfort in his statement—that someone would love me that much to rise up.

But then I realized I had no idea how my father would respond if he were here—how could I? The reality behind my uncle's statement washed over me as I wondered what my father really would have said had he been here. Then as if a veil was being removed, I began to question *how* or *if* my choices would have been different had my dad been alive. *What would growing up under his protection have felt like? Would I have been drawn to this complicated relationship had he been here to love me enough to defend me?*

I tried to dismiss the thoughts by remembering my mother's attempt to defend my honor, but instantly knew the failure lay in the reality that she is not my father. So as I sat in silence at the familiar round kitchen table, I closed my eyes and let my uncle's words penetrate a tucked away memory of a three year old who once twirled for her father. I savored the feeling that memorable look in his eye brought me and realized that, without warning, my uncle's spoken words were a candle illuminating an area in my life the years of void had threatened to consume in darkness. For the first time I identified the cost that came from being fatherless. And I wept.

Undoubtedly, it would be and take years before I would completely wrestle my heartache out with the Lord and understand what King David meant when he wrote, "A father of the fatherless, a defender of widows *is* God in His Holy habitation" (Psalm 68:5). But for now, all I knew to do was try and assemble the pieces I was being given. I had the Lord's promise that He would work all things together for my good, then Bob's gracious response to my pregnancy, and now this.

I left there that day a bit more perplexed than when I arrived but holding on to the truth behind my uncle's response. My father loved me even though he wasn't there to show it, and though I had no idea exactly the marker they would become, my uncle's words became the impetus behind a God ordained journey that would reveal the Father's love in such a way that it would forever alter the course of my life.

CHAPTER TWELVE

"The Best Laid Plans…"

–Robert Burns

THE LAST PERSON I still had to talk with was standing where he always stood, in front of the store, people watching. Gone was his flirtatious manner that had once captivated me, and in its place was a sternness that would have buckled my knees just a few days ago. But somehow the conversations that had occurred within the past 24 hours had strengthened my resolve and helped my legs to stand a bit straighter. So when he asked me if I had reached a decision, I didn't hesitate to tell him, "I'm having this baby."

I don't know if it was the frankness in which I spoke or if he was as weary as I was, but what I do know is that he didn't argue. He didn't waste time in telling me he wasn't in a position to help me, but he didn't present his case for an abortion either, which made me thankful. Instead, he just asked, "What do we do now?"

Admittedly, I didn't have any answers. I was caught in the crossfire of knowing he should be with his wife but wanting him to stay with me. I couldn't bear the thought of not having him, especially now, so without fully realizing it I made the decision that to have him in any capacity was better than not having him at all.

As winter ended and spring approached, news of my pregnancy broadened to more than just family. Although some of the students taunted and ridiculed me, the majority—who were perhaps shocked and angry at first—ultimately became a major source of emotional support for me my last few months of high school. These frequently were the same friends who had provided shelter for me in my earlier days of fleeing from my stepfather's house. None of them were overwhelmingly in favor of my relationship; it was me they supported.

Therefore, when news finally surfaced about his wife's pregnancy, my inner circle—both nearby and one state west—deeply challenged my ongoing refusal to terminate our relationship. I could hear the truth behind every "What is wrong with you?" or "How much of his behavior will you justify?"—none of which I had an answer for. I just knew I couldn't quit. I was like an addict and he was the fix that calmed my nerves, which meant I was willing to accept his "drug" on whatever terms I could get it. Walking away from him was simply not a viable option.

As graduation neared so did my imminent return to Indiana. I begged for a different course of action—I didn't want to leave him or Ohio, but with a baby on the way and no place to live I didn't have much choice. So, five days after receiving my high school diploma I packed my car and moved back to Indiana to wait for his wife to deliver their baby in August, then my own in October.

The eight weeks it took to reach the beginning of August passed by painstakingly slow. My relationship with my mother was strained at best if for no other reason than I was reluctant to place any component of my Ohio life beneath her scrutiny. I knew how she felt about him, so I could pre-formulate what her reaction would be to any mishap he and I may have had along the way. I believed since her objectivity no longer existed, neither did our relationship—at least not where he was concerned.

When the beginning of August finally arrived and his wife delivered their baby, I made a mental check on the calendar marking the first of three major events that needed to occur before I could move back to Ohio. I saw it as nothing more than a necessary step that had to take place in order for us to be together. Certainly the thought that he may actually love his wife was never even a remote possibility; after all, I was still holding on to the promise that he would finalize his divorce by the end of the year. And while I couldn't deny his diminishing number of phone calls, they weren't something I was willing to acknowledge, at least not verbally. Instead, when confronted, I justified his behavior by citing his hectic work schedule and a new baby.

Regardless of my mother's numerous concerns, I refused to give them any merit. I wasn't emotionally capable of validating her, but as the weeks passed by his waning interest was becoming harder and harder to ignore. I desperately missed our frequent phone conversations, and something about his distance just didn't feel right but no matter how often I asked him about it, he would repeatedly reassure me, "Kelly, we're fine. I'm just busy, that's all."

So, against all logic, I chose to believe him despite the fear that started to creep in. And when he promised to drive out so he could be there when I had the baby, I believed him. His words were salve to my soul, and even though I hung up desperately wanting everything to be exactly as he said, it was getting increasingly difficult to silence the still small voice that was beginning to say otherwise.

CHAPTER THIRTEEN
Deciding Factors

THE SMELL OF rustled leaves hung in the air as I searched for answers that most often eluded me. Still unable to reconcile what I believed was happening to my relationship with him, I chose instead to focus on the pressing need to make one last decision. The one choice still confronting me was whether to keep the baby or release him or her for adoption. Though months had passed since my initial decision for life, I still hadn't resolved this one final detail.

Most days I felt like a tennis ball being thrown back and forth; for every one reason to keep the baby, there were two that lobbed me back toward the adoption side of the court. And although his intentions were becoming increasingly more questionable, and I spent most of my days in the land of uncertainty, I still couldn't let go of his original plan. The idea of returning to Ohio, and to him, is what kept me functioning; I just had to decide if it would be with or without the baby.

These thoughts frequently kept my mind silently entertained, though there must have been moments when my mother saw brief opportunities to breach my private little world of well guarded secrets—but admittedly they didn't last long. She just happened to be wise enough to know exactly how to get in and the perfect time to get right back out. One such moment occurred while we sat eating lunch outside, enjoying the warmth of a fall day when she asked, "Kelly, have you made any decisions regarding the baby?"

I glanced down, rubbed my swollen belly, then squinted to look at her and said, "Not exactly. There's too much to think about."

The same look of compassion she had the night before the pregnancy was confirmed flashed in her eyes, and I wondered what she was thinking as she responded, "That there is," with more of a smirk than a grin.

I sat quietly, arching my head toward the sun, hoping she wouldn't ask me for more information; I never knew exactly what to say. Minutes passed in silence, then she said, "Well… you've narrowed your options, haven't you? You're either keeping the baby or giving it away, no?"

I just smiled at the obvious as she went on to explain, in much greater detail than before, what was really in store if I chose to keep the baby. She took her time in laying out a thorough plan by first acknowledging that while I was only 18, I would be required to get a job, then pay for the baby's daycare as well as pay half of the rent. She went on to explain that I would also have to help pay for the groceries and share the cost of the utilities, bringing her argument full circle, reiterating that while she knew I was only 18, I needed to understand what I was signing up for if I chose to keep the baby.

I tried to avoid showing any reaction, but she obviously had my attention. Up until now, my mind had been trying to understand what it meant to physically care for a baby 24 hours a day; I had never really thought about the financial aspects of my circumstances. I uttered a quiet, "Mmm, hmm," hoping she was finished. But then she added one more thing, that if I chose to go out with friends, I would need to hire a babysitter, reminding me one more time that she had already had her children and didn't intend on raising any more. She finished with the reassurance that if, at the end of the day, I was able to do all that she required then she would help me in any way she could.

I sat silent for quite awhile, stunned by the enormity of it all. "But Kelly," she said, "I don't know much about adoption, but if you want to go that route, I'll help you find out everything you'll need to know. And I'll be there then too, you must know that."

And then she went quiet as if she instinctively knew exactly when my door marked "Private" was going to close. She said as much as I could bear to hear, then gave me the room I needed to process.

I arched my head toward the sun and wished for the umpteenth time that it was all a bad dream. *How am I supposed to pay all that?* I wondered. Overwhelmed, I felt myself leap over the net toward adoption and instinctively knew that it represented some kind of freedom to me—certainly more freedom than what awaited me if I chose the parenting option. Yet, when I was brutally honest with myself this baby had, in just a short amount of time, come to represent so very much to me. He or she wasn't just a representation of a relationship I had completely sold out for; this baby represented my first step of soul survival. I heard the Lord first speak to me through this baby's presence. "I'm not sure I know how to let go of that," I mumbled to myself.

Then I thought about my mother. My mother, who no matter how I tried to ignore her, remained one of the strongest examples in my life. I glanced over at the woman sitting next to me and thought about how she defied her odds. I closed my eyes again and considered how she, despite facing insurmountable circumstances, had found a courage and tenacity unlike anyone I had ever known, to successfully feed, clothe and shelter all five of her children, all without ever wavering in letting us *know* we were loved.

If she could do that for five then how can I say no to one? I asked myself. It just didn't seem plausible to me; it was the one thing I could never seem to reconcile in my own heart. I thought about all she had said and it all felt so impossible, and then I realized, so did the whole situation. I tried to picture myself six months from now, alone and without this baby and I just couldn't picture it. Somewhere along the past eight months, every part of my life had become intertwined with that of this little being, and that's when I knew I couldn't let this baby go; he or she was mine, no matter what. And while I may not fully understand exactly what I was committing the next 18 years of my life toward, I somehow sensed that this decision was going to ultimately become a cornerstone to the foundation of my existence.

CHAPTER FOURTEEN

Surprises and Setbacks

NEARLY FIVE MONTHS had passed since I had returned to Indiana, and with each passing day it seemed as if my ties to Ohio were slowly being nicked away piece by piece. Regardless of his promise to be there when the baby was born, our phone conversations were becoming increasingly awkward as I would share things about my pregnancy and he would only respond with things about his other children. Still caught in the throes of emotional survival, I continued to keep those discussions to myself, finding it easier to mentally navigate the justification road and thereby convince myself things between us were normal.

Blind ignorance didn't just impact my emotions; it also made its contribution toward increasing the anticipation that comes with impending due dates and first time mothers. I was certain that every contraction was the beginning of labor, and although my mother was always there to reassure me they were probably Braxton Hicks contractions, I relentlessly made her time their length and frequency until ultimately they would mysteriously disappear through the same venue they had chosen to arrive. And with each false alarm, she was faithful to reassure me that we were just one step closer to the real thing.

Armed and ready through Lamaze classes, my mother and I faithfully practiced the breathing techniques, nightly anticipating the baby's arrival any day. I knew it was imminent, and I was scared to death. Although I had taken the classes and seen the film, the only source of sanity lay in the fact that when I looked at the other countless women who had already given birth, I took comfort in knowing they had all survived, which meant I should be okay.

It was early one October evening when I returned home from work, changed clothes and began talking with my mom as she prepared dinner when I felt a tightening across my stomach. Oddly different than the Braxton Hicks, I wasn't exactly sure if it was a contraction or if I just didn't feel well. Minutes passed, and each time the tightening sensation grew stronger, I was made more aware of their frequency. It took just a few hours before I was able to see for myself the difference between the two types of contractions and knew undoubtedly that these were for real. My mother, faithful with her notepad and pencil, timed the contractions according to the doctor's instructions until they grew close enough to warrant the trip to the hospital.

It was almost 11 p.m. before we got through hospital admissions and found ourselves in the labor room where we hee-hee'd and hoo-hooed our way through the ninety second contractions. Never leaving my side, my mother took every cleansing breath with me and counted through every transitional contraction until the doctor gave the okay to push. It was 5:40 a.m. when my firstborn took his first breath, and it was my mother who was the first to see him and welcome him into the world. Oddly enough, my son's arrival served as the final peacemaker between the invisible war that relationally existed between his mother and grandmother. It was in that moment when the union that naturally exists between a mother and her daughter was not only solidified but had become a fortress for this new life. There was no doubt that we were in this for the long haul together.

The next morning I anxiously waited for the clock to read 10 a.m. so I could make the most important phone call on my list. I had already presented the idea to my mom that he was coming out to see the baby, an idea she had reluctantly agreed to but was not overtly exuberant about. Regardless of her reaction, I was ecstatic and convinced that if she would just give him a chance, she would change her mind about him.

It was with that enthusiasm that I watched the clock tick until 10:05 a.m. and I knew he would be at work and could talk. The phone rang three times before he answered, and I was so excited to hear his voice. In response to my "Hello," he said, "Hey, what's up?"

It wasn't really disinterest I registered; it was more like I was an intrusion, which I quickly dismissed as my bad timing. So I pressed on, undeterred in my excitement. I shared with him about the baby—his length, his weight, and who he looks like. I shared all the things one is supposed to share with the father of her baby, but he casually replied, "Sounds just like my other two."

I fell quiet, stunned and unsure of how to respond to the ache that always seemed to surface lately whenever I talked with him. I sat silent, debating with myself whether or not to lash out in anger, knowing it was one thing for me to accept feeling slighted but questioning how a mother is supposed to respond when it's her child who gets the slighting; after all, I had only been a mother a few hours, it was all still too new. Choosing to say nothing, I listened as the awkward silence coursed between the phone lines until he mumbled something about not being able to come out; he "just couldn't get away right now."

Perhaps I should have been surprised but I wasn't; something deep inside of me feared this was forthcoming. Silence consumed me once again for I knew that if I pressed him on this issue, I risked him staying away for good, and that was something I couldn't bear to consider. So instead I swallowed both my anger and my disappointment and reluctantly whispered, "I understand."

I stared at the phone as it returned to its cradle, and for the first time, truly wondered what was wrong with me. *Why can't you stand your ground?* I asked myself, then laid my head back on the pillow and exhaled. *I'm so frustrated*, I thought—frustrated with him and his empty promises, and I was frustrated with myself. Then thoughts of the baby and everything I had planned for over the summer came back to me, and I wanted that life so badly I still wasn't ready to let go.

"He just needs to see us," I said to Silence, "then things will get back to normal." And once again I found myself injecting my emotional fix in whatever form I could get it.

CHAPTER FiFTEEN

The Power of a Name

A good name is to be chosen rather than great riches.
Proverbs 22:1

HAVING BELIEVED THAT he would come to Indiana when I delivered, I had promised myself I wouldn't name the baby until we were together. Yet here I sat in the hospital room and every time the baby was brought into me, the index card reading "Baby Boy" jumped out like flashing lights reminding me of unfinished business. For weeks prior to delivery, I had had the sense that the baby was a boy, and like most expectant mothers, had endlessly tossed around names. After much deliberation I had narrowed the options down and had decided that my favorite boy's name was Scott. Going into the delivery room I wasn't sure if his middle name would be Thomas, after my father, or Joseph who was a favorite grandfather of mine through our very blended family, but I was convinced that I loved the name Scott and would call the baby Scotty. It just seemed to fit.

Yet when I picked him up and allowed myself, despite the sickening disappointment that had taken residence from my earlier phone call, to absorb the moment and all that had occurred the past ten months, I found myself enthralled with his fair hair, his tiny mouth, his little fingers and ten toes. This moment, although undoubtedly designed to be shared by a mother and a father, had strangely become solely mine. And as my fingers traced the outline of his little face, I reflected on our journey and how dangerously close his existence came to being cut short.

I thought about the moment his "father" was missing, and sadness began to find its way into my soul—sadness for him and for me. But most importantly, sadness over the sheer fact that the thing that had caused some of the deepest torment in my own soul, my own lack of a father, was potentially what I would be passing on to my own son. I grieved over never having fully considered how my actions, or the complicated circumstances I now found myself in, would ultimately impact him. That alone broke my heart.

Reflecting back, that must have been where the first step toward truly becoming a mother was initially taken. Until then, my decisions had often come from a place of feeling like a pin ball; I bounced from thought to thought and primarily did whatever was expected of me. Confronted with the reality of potentially having inflicted the same pain I lived with, I vowed to protect this little life from the chaos that surrounded his existence. For the first time in what felt like a long time, I became proactive in a decision rather than reactive.

The fact that this life, not even 24 hours old, had already begun to change mine, amazed me, and through the intensity of the moment I began to discover the unique presence that rested on this little being—a presence that deserved to be identified by a name which would reflect its strength and tenacity. His name would have to hold substance and form because somehow this little guy had already beaten and defied his own odds.

So, with my head nestled in the pillow I closed my eyes and found myself welcoming my familiar companion Silence into the room. Untold minutes passed until slowly we embraced one another and began thanking God. I thanked Him for life... and for the moment...and for the honor. Then, like a quiet flutter that catches the corner of your eye, there was a pause or a catch in my spirit and I *knew* his name would not be Scott or Scotty. He didn't look like either one of those names; his essence was different.

I took another look at him and gently passed my thumb across the palm of his little hand, watching as his little fingers curled around my one. "Thank you, God," was all I could utter and like a momentary flash I remembered His promise to work all things together for my good. "He's such a blessing, Lord." And then it hit me that despite all that had happened, life is still a gift—therefore his name would be Matthew, for he was a gift from God. And the natural overflow would come from my beloved grandfather, Joseph.

Matthew Joseph would be his name, and I smiled for I was fully confident in the decision I had made. His name bore strength and meaning, and it was what I believed God had for him. Little could I foresee or truly know how very much he would come to inherit the full meaning of both of his names.

CHAPTER SIXTEEN

Desperate Times and Desperate Measures

THE NEXT FIVE weeks flew by as I adjusted to life as a single parent and struggled to come to terms with remnants of the frustration and anger I held toward Matthew's biological father's ongoing absence. For whatever reason, I failed to acknowledge what reality was trying to tell me and instead remained convinced that any damage done to our relationship over the past few months would be rectified if only he could see me and Matthew. So with every diaper change and midnight feeding, I recommitted myself to our original plan that was just weeks away from implementation; I told myself that if I could just hold on things would eventually return to normal. The only other thing I could do, in the meantime, was make as many weekend trips back to Ohio as possible.

Although I initiated the majority of our contact, the

strain that had become an expected part of our conversations seemed to somehow dissipate over the next six weeks. He was becoming more like his former approachable self and I, in turn, grew more and more encouraged. My emotions were directly correlated to his responses, and even though the actual time we spent together was limited, I remained completely pliable to him as if I was his loyal dog begging for a crumb—available whenever he created the time and space for that to happen. My addiction to his acceptance had robbed me of all my dignity and self respect, and the emotional stability that I took from whatever time he would spend with me was my sole goal in life. Therefore, when he was the one to ask if we could get together early evening on New Year's Eve, I was more than willing to say yes. Convinced this was the turning point from two long hard fought months of barely hanging on, I reveled in the thought of initializing our six month plan and began mentally strategizing the process of my permanent return to Ohio.

The dreariness of early winter greeted me as I pulled into his apartment complex. Gray and overcast, the sky seemed shrouded in uncertainty as occasional drops of precipitation melted on my windshield. Mounds of plowed snow created natural stop signs for the residents' cars, and the lake effect wind that often plagued northeast Ohio whipped the newly fallen snow across the pavement as I crossed the parking lot. *It seems like a good night to stay in, regardless of the holiday,* I thought, and with each step that took me closer to his door I silently planned another portion of our evening. *We'll catch up, have dinner, maybe watch a movie…then outline our plan for my return this spring. This is everything I've been waiting for*, I thought as I knocked on his door.

When the door opened and he greeted me with an awkward and distant hello, I wasn't sure how to respond. While cordial and polite, he acted like he didn't know what to say to me, as if we had nothing in common, and instead busied himself with idle jobs while my festive mood slowly seeped from my being. Unsure if I had done something wrong, I sat down without saying a word and waited for him to give me a cue so I could determine what I was supposed to say or how I was supposed to act. Moments later, in the midst of the stillness I recognized that Silence had somehow found his way in, and I immediately lost myself in his companionship, looking forward to the peace that always came with him.

When the room finally went altogether quiet, I looked up and watched as he put the last glass in the cabinet, hung up the dishtowel, then leaned on the counter and just looked at me. Unable to find any more deterrents, he stood there fidgeting, shifting his weight from one foot to the other until his efforts to stand still proved useless. Finally he sat down across the table from me, closed his eyes and blurted out, "We need to talk."

"Okay," I said, "Well…do you want to eat first?"

"No," he said, briefly lifting his eyes, "I have plans to eat later." Then barely above a whisper he said, "Let's just talk now."

I scanned his face, looking for some indication that would help reveal what could be bothering him but found nothing, so with uncertainty plaguing my soul and confusion wrinkling my brow I simply responded, "Okay."

He leaned forward in his seat and rested his hands on the

table, never once looking up. Mindlessly tracing his thumbnail with his finger, the struggle on his face betrayed the control he tried to convey in his voice. I watched as he fought to find the language that would explain how difficult the past seven months had been for him, how difficult they had been for all of us. Then I tried to make sense of the words that informed me he had made the decision to return to his wife.

An immediate barrier rose as I tried to guard my senses from an invisible assailant; I fought to not listen to his words, focusing instead on internally crying out for Silence to come and find me. But there I sat completely isolated, realizing that instead of strategizing how we would be together, I was listening to something that sounded incredibly like a defense argument detailing what life was like with his wife and their children, and how he realized he was no longer willing to finalize his divorce like he originally planned.

And then, as quickly as they had appeared, the sounds of the assault were over. He was done talking, and for the first time since I had knocked on the door he had the courage to actually look at me. Remnants of the past two years flashed through my mind as I struggled to catch my breath. I felt myself gasping for air, like his spoken words had given the command to turn off my life support against my will, and in a desperate act of survival I cried out, "You can't do this."

But I knew by the look on his face the fight was all but over. His eyes glistened with tears as he looked at me and whispered, "I'm sorry."

The chair legs screeched across the floor as I scooted back from the table in a futile effort to escape from the pain. "Please, please don't do this," I begged, aching for him to reconsider.

But his silence hung in the air revealing the dead end street I was walking, leaving me nowhere else to go. I sat silent, needing time to take it all in and absorb the fact that despite all of my best efforts, I was in the one place I never wanted to be—without him. After all that had happened I was alone, and the only two things I could think to ask were, "What am I supposed to do?... What about Matthew?"

When he didn't directly answer, my questions lingered, guiding me into virtually unknown territory. I was trapped in a mindless, emotional maze and believed that without him darkness would consume me. I glanced at him from across the table and reached for his hand in one last valiant effort to sway his decision, but all he could do was shy away from the table and say, "I can't," then repeat his apology.

I sat silent and stunned, numb from the enormous pain of it all. Had it only been a year since I was the college bound girl with the future at her door? I felt oddly old and worn out yet I was only 18. I tried to draw something from my internal well but had nothing left—no fight...no denial...no dignity.

The room grew silent as our emotions were gradually brought under control. I sat, the ticking of his clock marking the passing of time, and allowed the full reality of the situation to envelop me. It was all too surreal and the will to move evaded me, as if any movement would only serve to materialize that which had just been spoken. I figured if I could just sit there his words wouldn't carry as much weight so long as I didn't accompany them with an action. If I didn't leave, it wouldn't be over. Besides, I couldn't figure out how a dead person wills herself to move. I felt like my heart and soul had been blown to bits, and the only place I could find them was in the wadded up tissues that were now strewn across the table.

I waited for my breath to return to normal then slowly exhaled, knowing the inevitable was right in front of me. Glancing at the clock, I was struck by the thought of how quickly time can change things; funny how one can enter a room believing she completely belongs there and leave sometime later feeling like an uninvited guest. Sensing the new parameters, I finally looked at him and for the first time truly realized I didn't belong to this man or him to me—which meant, in my mind, I didn't belong to anybody. I had sold myself out for something that was never truly mine to have and had no way of redeeming that which had been lost along the way. So empty and void of all fight, I accepted his newly drawn boundary lines and conceded the battle.

It wasn't until I stood up and gathered my things that I recognized Silence had come to join me. Strengthened by his presence, I took a final moment to breathe it all in one last time, then walked over, kissed him on the cheek and with a silent nod of my head, I said goodbye.

CHAPTER SEVENTEEN

A New Normal

THE INTERNAL DARKNESS rolled like fog over my soul as I began my drive back to Indianapolis the next morning. Snippets of the life I had come to know over the past two and a half years replayed in my mind with each passing mile: times spent with friends, being on stage, meeting him, waiting for the pink circle to appear on the pregnancy test...on and on they rolled through my head as if someone or something had pressed the repeat button. I always believed that I would somehow find my way back to the life I had grown to love, and the sinking reality that there was nothing left of that life was unbearable. I kept waiting for the time to come when I would get a grip on my emotions, but whatever blackness had joined me in the car not only refused to leave, it felt like it had somehow stretched its talons down my throat and was trying to extract the core of my soul back out; I felt like I was being turned inside out. I couldn't breathe for its grip was too tight. The only release I found was through tears. There were no words, just countless tears that fell for everything that now only existed in my rearview mirror.

I knew that leaving Ohio this time was permanent, regardless of how much I fought it. There was truly nothing to return to; my friends had gone on to college and he had gone back to his wife. And then there was Indiana—always beckoning me, despite my constant refusal to accept it. I found it funny that the road that lay ahead of me represented my future when all I really wanted to do was turn my car around and head back to my past.

No sooner would the memories and their partnered emotions subside then the plaguing thoughts of my own ignorance would begin their assault: *If I had known better ... or ... If I had chosen differently, then... Then what?* I couldn't answer myself. I just knew I was completely ill-prepared for paying the high cost that my decisions had brought. I knew that choosing life and parenting would be pricey, but I had comforted myself with the idea that I would be back in Ohio and we would be together, just like we planned. I never prepared or budgeted for being by myself or for losing everything I cherished about my life—him, my home, my friends—my entire existence. I never anticipated my choices would require me to forfeit everything that ever mattered to me. I just didn't know.

I was half-way to Indianapolis when Silence rejoined me on my journey. We sat for quite awhile together finding comfort through the radio and its ability to act as a mental time machine. Consumed in my own thought life, my cognitive consolations were politely interrupted by Silence who drew my attention toward a fellow passenger, one whom I had never met before but I somehow knew I would be spending a fair amount of time with in the near future. Silence politely introduced me to Sorrow who, from what I could tell, had no end. He was just there, ever present—my new loyal friend. And as I mindlessly drove back to Indianapolis, my two unseen companions were faithful to ride right along with me.

CHAPTER EIGHTEEN

Freedom for the Captive

And you shall know the truth and the truth
shall make you free.
John 8:32

THE MONTHS THAT followed my return to Indianapolis held
no light; they were mechanical and lifeless. Food had no
flavor, my surroundings no color, and emotions no feeling
except for Sorrow, who was always there. My mind had
no thought for I would often silently wonder who dressed
Matthew, only to discover that countless actions of mine were
less than memorable to me. They were just thoughtless acts of
necessity, why would one remember them?

Life had become a battleground for existence; I struggled
to care. With everything and everyone gone, I questioned why
or if things truly mattered. Whether my eyes were opened
or closed, whether I was there or not, the situation wouldn't

change—he wasn't coming back. The only constant I did have was Sorrow; I couldn't avoid his companionship, no matter how rudely I behaved.

Over time Sorrow, like Silence, had friends that he wanted to share with me. However, these "friends" were different; they were a bit shadier and of questionable character. Sorrow slowly opened the door for Fear and Shame to enter into my realm of existence. So there I was consumed with a sadness that threatened to envelop my soul, confined to a world where I was startled by my own shadow, and the only escape I could find was to hide from anyone or anything that was unfamiliar to me.

The sole place I felt sheltered from the onslaught of peoples' presumed stares and silent accusations was in the shadow of my mother. She had become my shield and defender, the person I literally hid behind when out in public. Never wanting to be the person that stood out in a crowd or the exception to the rule, peoples' silent criticism and potential rejection had grown into undefeatable assailants, and I no longer had the emotional stamina to protect myself. My affiliation with Fear had begun to slowly paralyze me, and like a seeping menace, my fear of vulnerability just made it easier to remain inside if my mother wasn't with me.

The ensuing darkness made both my mother and sister desperate for intervention, and they were tireless in their efforts to permeate my world of despair. They confronted, consoled, invited and fought valiantly to find a way to snap me out of my emotional abyss. There were often times that I would watch them enjoying one another, and although I would be sitting right next to them, I felt completely removed from their presence. Undoubtedly the lightness of their relationship would cause something to spark in my spirit, as if I was in the middle of a cave and could see a pinhead light far, far off in the distance. However, no sooner would the light flicker then it would get blown out and I was once again left in the dark, consoled only by my newfound "friends," convinced the only safe place for me to be was inside the protected blackness of emotional isolation.

I wasn't capable of finding my way out of the cave; most often I didn't have what it took to lift my hands so I could grope my way around. I just didn't have the energy required to take the first step; there was nothing left. Instead, I would become enveloped by the vortex of blackness, void of shape and order, and any ray of light that attempted to penetrate the dark would immediately get snuffed out through my own unspoken fear of being out in the open where there was light and the air was fresh.

By summer, I had become a physical shell of my former self, unable or unwilling to eat; nearly twenty pounds had fallen off my five foot frame, and I looked skeletal. Thoughts of inferiority plagued me as I began convincing myself that if I had been thinner, perhaps he wouldn't have left. Certainly his departure was caused because *I wasn't skinny enough* or *good enough* or . . . . . whatever thought filled in the blank on any given day. The thoughts were relentless in their torment. My physical appearance had become a true manifestation of where I was emotionally: wane and completely deficient. Perhaps through reflection, I have come to understand that eating, or the lack thereof, was the one thing I was able to control in a world that for me had spiraled out of control. Regardless of motivation, it was becoming more and more obvious that I was slipping dangerously close toward a world out of which no one could extract me.

There were moments during those summer days when I truly questioned if I would ever be "normal" again or if my existence would always be viewed through the cloud of thick darkness. It wasn't as if I was enjoying the state of my life or what I had become; it was more like I was trapped in a maze and felt that no matter which direction I turned, I couldn't escape from the pain that continually ravaged my soul. It was as if it had claws like a cat that hung on a tree; its grip kept sinking deeper and deeper into me no matter how I or anybody else tried to free me from the pain.

As Matthew's first birthday approached, my mother's concern began to border on sheer desperation. Not only was she an eyewitness to my internal struggles, she had become a supporting cast member with her own part to play, and that part required an enormous emotional investment from her. Not one to live without clear boundary lines, it was an early Saturday morning after a recent move to the city's west side when she asked to speak with me. So with boxes still unpacked and breakfast barely over, I got Matthew situated with his toys and sat down.

Noting that it had been almost ten months since he told me he was returning to his wife, she simply asked me, "Kelly, how long do you think you can keep going on like this?"

The stark reality of her question made me barely able to look at her, as if the light was too bright and although my mind frantically sought an answer, there was none to be found. My only thought was to cry out, "If I knew how to feel differently,

I would." But I didn't. Silence surfaced, so I just stared at her. I had no words. Instead I nervously bit my lip and wondered how one is supposed to feel when a cavern-sized hole has taken the place of her heart?

She went on, "Kelly, something has to change."

I knew she was right but I couldn't speak. The silence grew increasingly awkward and I was feeling cornered, like I was a trapped animal. Suddenly things went very dark and I found myself back in the cave unable to see the pinhead light at the end of the tunnel, which frightened me because this fear, unlike that which drove me into hiding, felt like it was inescapable. I tried to fight against the blackness as it began to roll over and threaten me once more, realizing that it felt like I was being held captive and silenced by my corrupt friends. If I didn't find the courage or strength to scream for help this blackness would forever engulf me in its presence. So for the first time in ten months, I found the will to fight for my voice. In just seconds my stutters and gasps for air filled the room, as if a small dam had been unlocked and out gushed the questions, "What if I always feel like this? Wh..wh..what if I never get better? What if … I can't find my way out?"

My mother held my hands as I laid my head on the table and let my brokenness come to the surface. Months of pent up, unspoken emotion came pouring out from the deepest places of my soul. His rejection, my loss of innocence, the subsequent unending pit of sorrow that I lived with were all spewed out in front of my mother. And when the worst of it was over and she knew I could listen, she simply asked me, "Kelly, after losing my first husband, do you know what the one thing was that consistently got me out of bed every day?"

Silenced by emotion, I could only shake my head no.

"I told myself that it doesn't hurt as much today as it did the first day he died, which meant I was surviving. . . barely… but at least I was surviving."

She went on, "In other words, Kelly, the days of your worst pain are really behind you. It doesn't hurt as bad today as it did when you first found out, does it?"

I sat silent, taking time to measure the pain with her verbal yardstick. I analyzed the first days of returning to Indiana and the absolute barrenness that had surrounded my life, then I compared those feelings to where I was that morning, that early Saturday the first of October, and found hope in the measurable difference. Like a physical wound that has begun to heal, I could see where the original damage had occurred and yet recognized that the scab had somehow slowly begun to form.

I thought about where I had been and began to explore the reality that while I was still consumed with boundless amounts of pain, she was right; I couldn't be found in the tissues on his table because I wasn't completely blown into pieces anymore. On the contrary, some parts had actually begun to reattach and therefore function. And while I wondered how long it would take before I would be completely whole again, I was able to recognize that the talons that at one time felt as if they would never let go had indeed begun to loosen their grip.

CHAPTER NINETEEN
Masked Men and Other Superheroes

THE YEAR FOLLOWING my mother's cry of truth brought with it a gradual broadening of the light that had previously only existed in the far distance of the cave, as if it was beckoning me to come closer to the cave's opening. As I finally began surfacing for air, I discovered food was beginning to share its flavor, and life as a whole no longer felt like it was happening in black and white; rather, through each experience I was being given an opportunity to paint a small portion of my own paint by numbers project.

I was relearning how to dwell outside the protective walls of my self-created cave because I still deeply struggled to venture very far into the land of unfamiliar, especially without my mother. Even though it had been almost a year since we had moved to the west side and I had grown somewhat independent in my routine of working and going to Matthew's babysitter, I remained ever mindful of the fear that would grip me everywhere else if I dared wander too far away from her presence. Without her, I was completely vulnerable and would become consumed with the driving need to seek shelter back in the darkness of the cave where I felt protected and unexposed.

My mother allowed me to cling to her until the following spring, just before my 21st birthday. That's when she decided she needed to find a way to lure me out of the cave without her being near. She randomly and without any warning began sending me out on small errands, all the while refusing to go with me. When she first asked me to go, I adamantly refused and trembled at the thought of people looking at me and not having her there to hide behind. She persisted though until she broke through my resolve, which allowed me to discover that every time I went out alone and returned successful in my mission, the more courage would embolden me. It wasn't long before I recognized that Fear and Shame were no longer constricting my throat and, despite their subtle ongoing presence, I was learning to live fairly comfortably on the outskirts of the cave.

The same lightness that was gradually seeping back into my existence seemed to permeate our home environment as well. My mother, sister and I had established a workable routine and had grown quite comfortable with operating interdependently. I felt safe within the confines of our relationships and our respective routines. And, like most single parents, each of us worked all week and looked forward to the leisure of weekends. The only weekend requirement was an agreement to attend the local Christian church just down the street, so every Sunday my mother drove my sister, me and our two boys, making this a natural part of our life. And like always, I found security in the mindless routine of my sister and me walking our boys to their respective Sunday school rooms while our mother secured our seats in her self-established place: five pews back from the altar, just left of center, right on the end.

There is an unexpected comfort that comes from knowing exactly what to expect from people, and feeling comfortable at church was something that didn't take long to establish. Perhaps it was Matthew's unusual interest in the Bible stories or the extraordinary kindness of the workers each time I dropped him off, but I could never quite understand why I rarely felt the need to guard against Fear and Shame's unwelcome appearance when I was there. It was one of the few places where I felt secure enough to let my guard down, despite being the only one of hundreds of parents who was single.

While church attendance quickly became a Sunday morning ritual, it somehow seemed to hold a newness to it every weekend. Albeit the physical routine was the same, it was the spiritual side that remained a bit unpredictable, and that was all I needed for my sense of awareness to increase every time I walked into the auditorium.

Inevitably as my sister and I would enter the double oak doors of the sanctuary, my eyes would quickly scan to find my mother and secure the path we would take to get to her. The church itself was enormous, able to seat over 1,500 people and walking the long aisle was never a favorite activity of mine. I could feel peoples' penetrating stares through the back of my head as I traversed my way to my mother's pew, and no matter how quickly I willed my legs to go I could never seem to get to her fast enough.

Finally, once my sister and I inched ourselves around my mother's legs, I sat back and exhaled, content to be seated and lost within the mix of hundreds of people. I scanned the bulletin, wondering if they (whoever "they" are) found as much security in routine as I did because we always sang the same number of hymns and took communion at the same time, right before we heard the sermon—all very routine and predictable. I knew I could relax and find solace in knowing what to expect until the end of service when the pastor presented the opportunity for people to be baptized. We stood as we always did, singing our way toward the middle verses of the Invitational Song when I felt my sister's elbow nudge the left side of my rib cage and then heard her whisper, "Look," almost with a grunt.

"What?" I whispered in response.

As she subtly nodded her head toward the aisle, I turned my neck quickly backward to see a young man walking down the aisle toward the front of the church. Like a magnet my eyes watched each deliberate step he took to get to the head pastor, and for countless seconds my sense of sight was all that seemed to work. Something about him, perhaps his obvious good looks, hit me with such an unexpected force that I was struck stupid and could think of nothing to say except to ask my sister, "Who is that masked man?"

Much to my mother's chagrin our ensuing giggles carried us through the end of service until it was time to make our way toward our Sunday school class. Recognizing that I had been knocked slightly off kilter by my reaction to this morning's visitor, I tried to lose myself in conversation with my sister but was acutely aware of my "friends" Fear and Shame and their ominous threat of an unwelcome appearance. I tried to ignore their subtle acts of intimidation by adhering myself to either my sister or my mother, never venturing far off on my own. Everything in me began warning me to run back into the cave, and as my heartbeat started to echo in my ears and my breath began to shorten, I fought to stay focused on their respective conversations until my mother, noticing the "masked man" from service, suddenly excused herself and went to be the class's sole member of the welcoming committee.

I stood there alone, without a clue as to what to say to the people she had been speaking with, and within minutes found myself inept and blundering as I tried to politely answer their questions. I stammered and stuttered as I was rendered inattentive to their efforts. Instead my mind wondered why, out of all the classes he could have gone to, had he picked this one. *Really?* I indignantly questioned. I looked up and realized that the only thing worse than not knowing what to say is to be left alone in a roomful of people who had obviously found countless things to talk about with everybody but you. I wanted to scream, "I have no friends!" and desperately longed for the security of the cave. I felt completely exposed and vulnerable, but this time was worse because I couldn't seem to even find the opening of the cave. My eyes, almost uncontrollably, began scouring the room searching for a way out. I wanted to be alone. Silence was the only one who knew how to accompany me when things got like this, but in the midst of all the noise and confusion I couldn't find him either.

With my head down I began to inch my way toward the back wall, hoping no one would notice. Just then out of the corner of my eye I saw my mother move toward me, as if her internal radar had gone off and she knew I was in some kind of trouble. I leaned back on the wall, tucking my hands behind my back and tried to catch my breath, focusing my eyes on a fuzz ball three feet in front of me. When I sensed her next to me, I cautiously looked up and allowed her presence to cement the ground underneath me. "Kelly, are you okay?" she asked.

With the worst of it suddenly behind me, I grinned, closed my eyes and hesitantly said, "Yeah, I'm fine."

"Good," she said smiling, "because there's somebody I'd like you to meet."

And with that, she took my hand and walked me over to the doorway where the masked man stood talking to other members of the class. I made every effort to pull my hand away from hers so I could find my way back to the wall, but the harder I pulled, the tighter she gripped until I accepted her silent message to "stay put."

The balls of my feet burned as I stood there, my mother's hand like a vice grip around my fingers, and though I tried to stand still I fidgeted like a toddler impatiently waiting for her parents to finish talking. It wasn't until people started taking their seats and the doorway cleared out that I heard my mother say, "Well, Randy, I wanted you to meet my youngest daughter, Kelly."

It took everything I had to look up at him and, much like I felt earlier that morning, I was unexpectedly struck by the force of his presence. Instantly I felt his eyes bore through all my fabricated layers as if he could see into the depths of my being; every emotion and wound I had was completely exposed and bare for him to see. I frantically searched for a way to emotionally cover my transparency but I didn't know how; all I could do was look away to find relief from those penetrating eyes. But when he asked me a question and I looked back to answer, what frightened me more than being exposed was the tenderness I saw in him.

If he saw what it felt like he could see then why did he have so much compassion, I wondered. *Why didn't I see reproach or contempt in his eyes?* Instead, I saw the deepest pools of something...*but what?* Looking at him was like having lightning course through me; there was an electricity that surrounded the space we were standing in, and I immediately felt overwhelmed with the need to once again find shelter from the exposure. I couldn't think, and my jumbled up emotions felt like a noose tightening around my neck. I tried looking everywhere but at him, then gurgling out a response, I mumbled something about it being time to find my seat, then quickly turned to sit with my sister.

The remainder of our time spent at church was a mechanical exercise of survival. Without saying another word I left the class, picked up Matthew and quickly walked to the car. It wasn't until we were on our way home that Silence finally decided to join me as I became lost in my own thoughts. Every time I closed my eyes all I could see were those eyes of his invading my line of defense, making it impossible to protect myself. So instead I stared out the window, half listening to Matthew as he sang about his favorite Bible character, "Zacchaeus, the wee little man," the other half of me trying to understand why my mother felt the need to extend a dinner invitation to this man whose presence caused such emotional upheaval for me.

I resisted the urge to argue with her logic because I knew I was completely outnumbered; my sister had already declared she wanted to see if he would be "fun to talk to." Therefore I chose to let Silence work me through my frustration toward my mother's generosity and then decided that, regardless of how handsome or tender his eyes appeared, I would not let this man, this "Randy," have any more access into my very structured, very well protected world. I promised myself...no matter what.

CHAPTER TWENTY

Suspicious Alliances

IN ADDITION TO dinner plans my mother decided that entertainment should be part of the evening's experience, so she prepared for a "foursome" on the local tennis courts. I complained, protested and valiantly resisted any thought of joining in the role of hospitality, to which my mother chided me, saying, "Kelly, I'm surprised at you. He is a new Christian after all, and we're just trying to be welcoming."

Unable to forget the effect of his penetrating stare, I rolled my eyes at her and silently told myself, *Whatever.* When the doorbell rang later that afternoon, Randy was greeted by another small welcoming committee. Extroverts by nature, my mother and sister have never really known a stranger and meeting Randy was no different for them. They immediately invited him in and made him feel right at home. I, on the other hand, was quite content to remain in my highly limited social world where things were very orderly and controlled.

After all, I was still learning how to effectively live outside of the security I felt in my cave. The thought of venturing too far from its opening was completely paralyzing, and talking with him felt as if I was *way* out in the open. Thus I remained seated on the living room floor seemingly lost in Matthew's crayons and coloring book, and only glanced at him when I thought he wasn't looking; exposure was just not going to be an option.

It wouldn't be until years later that I would truly understand the heart behind his initial efforts of trying to break through my carefully laid out defense system. There was no doubt that, from my perspective, he was an unwanted trespasser who shouldn't be trusted. Based on my earlier encounter with him at the church, he was a threat to the barriers that I had erected around Matthew and me. Without warning he had somehow been able, and with seemingly little effort, to scale the walls I had built to avoid any and all heartache. Yet it seemed no matter what silent barriers I erected, Randy remained steadfast in his pursuit of breaking through them.

Within minutes of acknowledging and thanking my mother for having him, he navigated his way into the living room, bent down at his knees and waited for me to look up. Bracing myself for those pools of tenderness, I willed my eyes to glaze over so he couldn't see my emotional disarray, and in a split second looked up at him and right back down, hoping for some distraction to overshadow my vulnerability. I watched as Matthew's little hand struggled to fit his crayon back into the back row of his tiered Crayola box. Then looking up, he said, "Hi, I'm Matt. Do you love God and Jesus? If you do, I can be your friend."

That first greeting from an almost three year old nearly knocked Randy off his feet, and I couldn't help but become a silent observer to their conversation. Randy quickly smiled at Matt and said, "As a matter of fact I do…very much."

Then with the slightest of pause he continued, "Hi, my name is Randy," which was just enough of a distraction for me to forget that I had momentarily stepped further away from my cave's opening than I had in a long time. But it was only for a few seconds because in the brief moment it took for me to venture out, I discovered that for the second time in one day Randy had somehow not only penetrated my defenses, but he had gotten to Matt, causing instant reinforcement of my fortress and skepticism of his intent to fester in my soul.

The onset of my coldness was nearly immediate, and I chose to spend the rest of the day mindlessly going through the motions of lobbing the tennis ball back and forth—then home for dinner. It was early evening when, despite my quiet insistence to spend time with Silence, my sister and mother had somehow successfully elected me to walk Randy back to his car. Awkward and desperate to run back into my cave, I listened as he tried to ease the tension by sharing some of his story and what led him to the church. While I had compassion for his story, I had no words to encourage conversation. I was an emotional vault, unwilling to share anything about myself and he was too much of a gentleman to come right out and ask. So he concluded the evening by asking me to thank my mother again for all she had done, then we both said good night.

As I made my way back to the house, sounds of their laughter rolled through the open door as I re-entered our home.

There was a soft spring breeze blowing the kitchen curtains as my mother stood at the sink reviewing the day's events with my sister. I glanced toward the boys playing in the living room but my ears were honing in on my mother's voice, stating, "He is such a nice guy."

"I know," my sister said. "I enjoyed getting to know him a little."

My mother, always looking for someone to nurture, replied, "Yeah, we'll have to have him over again."

I stood there exasperated with their intent on repeating the day's plans and wondered what it was exactly they saw in him. *How could they be so enamored already*, I wondered, fighting the urge to walk in there and say, "I don't trust him, no one is that nice without having an ulterior motive." But instead I decided to stand still, keeping my thoughts to myself, and took comfort in telling Silence, *They can get to know him all they want, I'm not interested.*

As I turned to go upstairs the last comment I heard my mother utter was, "All I know is that I don't care which of my daughters marries him, but one of you will. He's too good to let go."

I rolled my eyes and for the second time that day told Silence, *whatever.*

CHAPTER TWENTY-ONE

Risk Factors

THE NEXT FEW months bore witness to my 21st birthday, Matthew turning three and, much to my disapproval, frequent dinner invitations being extended to Randy. There was no doubt that the more my mother invited him, the more I resisted and shunned his presence. I treated him in similar fashion to the way I once treated Sorrow when I returned from Ohio; he was an unwelcome visitor and I tried my best to disassociate myself from him.

But regardless of how rudely I treated him, Randy didn't seem to get the hint. On the contrary, though the majority of his time was spent talking with my mother and sister while I occupied myself in another room, he invariably would call a day or two later asking me to go somewhere, and I would always respond with a quick but emphatic no.

After weeks of his pursuit and my subsequent denials, my

mother began indirectly questioning my judgment. "He's so nice, Kelly. Just try and go with him one time."

To which I faithfully responded, "If he's so nice, let Lauren go out with him. I'm not interested."

And then, as if on cue and rehearsed, Lauren would holler from the other room, "No, thank you. We're just friends, he's not my type."

I tried to avoid showing any sign of weakness, but the reality was I felt stuck—or worse yet, trapped. I was convinced I wasn't interested, yet I felt a certain amount of pressure from my mother and in constant pursuit by a man who would not take no for an answer no matter how many times he heard it. My mother liked him, my sister liked him and Matthew liked him—I didn't. Besides, he was still viewed as a security threat.

The first of July brought with it Indy's annual Jazz Festival, and sure enough the phone rang mid week prior to the event. After the second ring I heard my mother call, "Kelly, it's Randy. He'd like to talk with you."

Completely frustrated with her tenacity, I approached the phone mouthing, "Why didn't you tell him I'm not home?" She merely smirked, shrugged her shoulders and handed me the phone.

Immediately after saying hello, Randy—always the gentleman—identified himself, which completely incited me for I already knew it was him on the phone, so I bit my tongue trying to avoid being completely rude. He continued unaware of my self-constraint and asked me how I was doing, how was Matthew, etc., while I grew exceedingly impatient to end the conversation. I briefly and abruptly answered his questions, but refused to ask him anything that could prolong our dialogue.

Gradually maneuvering his way toward the point of his call, he invited me to attend the Jazz Festival that Saturday with him and another couple. I shook my head wondering, *What will it take for this guy to get the point?* Lost in my own thoughts about his assumed "ignorance," I disengaged from his verbal itinerary of what the evening would look like if I said yes and instead started the process of mentally formulating my case for saying no. But then, as if the thought had leapt in front of me stopping me dead in my tracks, I actually contemplated the idea of how to avoid disappointing anyone, especially my mother.

Her words about him began to suddenly reemerge in the back of my head, getting louder with each silent utterance, and then like a rolling snowball, the idea of possibly going out with him, just one time, might cause him to relent and then everyone would leave me alone about it. Then when I said no to future invites, I could always say I tried. I listened as he rambled on, and before I lost my nerve, quickly exhaled louder than intended, closed my eyes and said, "Okay."

Early that following Saturday, as we traveled back from the Chicago area to celebrate the 4th, memories of his piercing eyes began to consume my thoughts. I was hours away from going out with the one man to whom I felt completely exposed, and that reality sent me into a whirlwind of conflicting emotions. For the first time in a long time, I allowed thoughts of Ohio and what it was like to become completely vulnerable resurface, then remembered the piercing pain that accompanied my exodus back to Indiana. The subsequent raw existence that defined those early months after rushed to join my mental movie, and I instantly knew I couldn't go back there. Regardless of how much my mother had encouraged me or how nice of a guy my sister thought he was, there was no way I could follow through with going out with him, no matter how good of a plan I concocted. The reality was that my capacity to trust anyone, regardless of how genuine they may seem, had been destroyed. I had worked too hard this past year learning how to live outside my captivity. I just wasn't willing to risk returning to my earlier cave days of existence; I would rather live my life alone.

Subsequently, I resolved that as soon as my mother pulled the car into our designated parking spot and I helped unload our things I would make my phone call, even if it was a last minute cancellation. I had made my decision and promised myself I wouldn't go out with Randy—not then, not ever. He was just too great a risk.

CHAPTER TWENTY-TWO

A Matter of the Will

THE DAYS FOLLOWING my last minute cancellation turned into weeks, and before I knew it the weeks had somehow turned into months. To my delight the phone had finally quit ringing and Randy's visits had slowly started to taper off until he ultimately ceased coming over. Without the unspoken pressure looming all around, I found myself able to refocus my attention on Matthew and securing our world of limited exposure.

Contentment in my routine and solitary life eventually returned, and while I hardly ever dated, if I did it was only with someone who represented no actual threat to my predictable existence. I had discovered that the easiest and safest way to maneuver through life was to live on a highly surface level and if someone or something threatened to penetrate my façade, retreat was easily found in the shelter of motherhood and my other responsibilities. Life offered as much entertainment as

I chose to take, and so long as I maintained authority over the parameters, Fear and Shame were demoted to being just distant acquaintances.

By the time November arrived our church had begun preparing for its upcoming revival, and like most special gatherings at the church, there was a silent understanding that all five of us would attend. And, as usual, our agenda that first night of the revival looked very similar to the one we carried out every Sunday morning: my sister and I would take the boys to their respective rooms for childcare while my mother would procure our self assigned seats: five pews back from the altar, just left of center, on the end.

In my mind, this was the one routine that was bittersweet…I thoroughly appreciated the guarantee that I would have a seat as soon as I walked into the sanctuary, enabling me to avoid being left standing alone, feeling like everyone was looking at me and wondering why I didn't have any friends. The downside was, however, it also meant I was easily identifiable, which was incredibly nerve wracking since I preferred being covert and unseen.

Navigating through my mental duplicity kept my attention as my sister and I entered through the massive double oak doors leading into the sanctuary. Always on the lookout for predators, my eyes quickly scanned the numbers of people I would have to walk in front of as I descended toward my mother's pew. We were half way down the aisle when my sister happily said, "Oh look, Randy's here."

Bracing myself for his typical visual invasion of my fortress, I stopped dead in my tracks and frantically said, "Where?"

My sister, calmly taking my hand, kept walking and without looking at me, said, "Look, right next to mom."

"Great," I murmured, "What's he doing there?" I asked more rhetorically than really wanting an answer. As we continued to inch our way toward the front of the church, my blood started to rapidly course through my veins, sending sounds of militant heartbeats pounding in my ears. The hand my sister was holding grew clammy and sweaty as my survival instincts screamed for me to turn and run the other way. By the time we actually got to the pew where they were seated, I had worked myself up into such a frenzy that all I could offer them was an indistinctive grunt in place of a hello and propel myself to the furthest available seat away from him.

Thankfully my mother chose not to play matchmaker that evening, keeping Randy on her right side as I allowed my actions to convey that there was no way I was sitting any closer to him than absolutely necessary. Desperate to keep my inner world safe from exposure, I reminded myself that he was an unwelcome intruder in my world, which completely exasperated me. I sat down feeling frustrated and invaded, sullen at the thought that just about the time I believed he had got my message and was going to leave me alone, here he was again.

Like a little girl who sulked because she couldn't get her way, I slouched down in the pew, crossed my arms and found myself internally groaning at my predicament. Instead of listening to the pastor preach about the goodness of God, all I really heard was the phrase *Now what?* course through my mind. I fixed my eyes straight ahead, not willing to even remotely glance sideways for fear of seeing those eyes staring back at me until at last the service was over, freeing me to exit the row opposite of the way I came in and go pick up Matthew.

Night after night for the next five consecutive evenings the same thing occurred. The only difference was that after the initial shock of seeing him in our pew the first night, I was prepared to see the back of his head the other evenings. So as my sister and I would round the corner of the double doors, I willed my eyes to glaze over so he couldn't see what lay beneath my surface.

On Tuesday evening, the third night of the revival, when my sister and I entered the sanctuary I immediately noticed that he wasn't sitting on my mother's right. Giving a premature exhale I started to relax at the thought of not having to guard against his presence but then quickly realized that I didn't look long enough. Seeing my mother on the end of the aisle, I assumed he wasn't there but when I looked more closely, I realized that while he wasn't on her right he was indeed seated on her left, leaving room for only one person to sit between him and me—my sister. I sighed, glancing over at her as we walked down the aisle and said, "He moved."

Irritated, she curtly responded, "What?"

"He moved," I said. "He's not on the aisle. He's closer," as if his physical proximity was directly correlated to the emotional access he might gain with me. Feeling as if this was all happening way too fast, I frantically began searching for some way to establish some distance from his presence. I froze and looked for an open seat anywhere other than where he was. Tuned into my apprehension and subsequent paralysis, my sister rolled her eyes, loudly exhaled, and grabbed my hand saying, "Oh, come on. You're fine."

As we inched and excused our way into the pew I sheepishly looked up at him, uttered a fast hello, and then quickly took my seat next to my sister. Scanning the bulletin, I must have read the same paragraph three times before I finally laid it on the seat next to me and fidgeted my way toward the beginning of the service. However, no matter how much effort I made to pay attention, I found myself feeling like I had been transported back to that May afternoon when everyone was in the living room and all I could do was try to sneak peeks at him when he wasn't watching. Sitting in that pew stealing glimpses of him as he listened to the preacher was an intriguing exercise in a covert operation; I was beginning to find his conduct somehow disarming and fascinating. By the end of the evening I found myself actually able to say an audible good night, then excuse myself to go and pick up Matthew.

Moments later, after most of the people had already left, I heard my sister approach as I bent down to gather Matthew's things. Standing next to me, she listened as Matthew explained his latest craft, watching as his little fingers traced the outline of his boat. It wasn't until I bent down to zip up his coat that my sister looked at me and said, "So, I've noticed you've been a little nicer to Randy. Is he growing on you?"

As if hit with a blinding light you can't directly look at, I immediately closed my eyes as part of me reared back wanting to return to the security and quietness of my cave...but yet there was another part of me that instinctively knew I was being drawn to him by some unrecognizable and irresistible force. I smirked at the thought, then opened my eyes and stood up. I looked at her and shrugged, not ready to fully admit to his allure. "Maybe," I said playfully, and turned to walk out the door, taking Matthew with me.

For the last time that week, my sister and I rounded the corner and entered through the double doors, immediately finding our mother and Randy sitting in the pew. A bit more confident about how to stand my ground, I didn't freeze in place or mutter unwelcoming questions under my breath; instead I just kept walking. This time, however, it was my sister who inched and excused herself into the row first, leaving me to sit right next to Randy.

The nearness of his presence consumed my every thought. It was as if an accidental brush from him would send electrical shocks through me; the only saving grace I had was he was fixed on the preacher's sermon and seemingly not paying attention to me or my reactions. I mentally explored how this evolution occurred but came up with little to no answers. I just knew that what intrigued me about this man was far greater than my desire to retreat back into my cave.

After our home pastor finished the closing prayer of the evening and we began collecting our things, I heard my mother say, "Randy, would you like to come over and join us for some hot chocolate?"

I watched my mother's eyes drift from looking at him to finding me. Then, as the question hung in the air waiting for his response, I felt his eyes search mine as if he needed me to be okay with the idea. For the first time since I met him, not an ounce of resentment rose up in me. On the contrary, I felt relaxed and comfortable with the idea so I simply shrugged my shoulders as if to say it doesn't matter, and went back to collecting my things. I felt his attention shift back toward my mother as I heard him say, "Yeah, that would be great. Thank you."

Living minutes from the church, it didn't take long before Randy arrived and I was once again caught up in the intrigue his presence created. Even amid all the commotion of my mother's preparations and two toddlers rambling on about what they had learned at church, I was acutely aware of the gentleness in which he responded to the ensuing noise and chaos. And although I was growing more comfortable with the idea of his being there, I was also equally aware that at some point Silence had come to join me at the table too, quietly reassuring me of his protection and covering.

I sat primarily as a silent listener to the conversation, not overtly eager to say too much but pleased that I could at least sit at the table and not feel the need to burrow back into a hole. I lingered there, recognizing that even my breathing was stable and consistent. In fact, the longer I sat there the more I realized the relational pressure I once felt so real had somehow dissipated over the course of the past week, and I no longer felt the requirement to come out of hiding; rather unknowingly, I found myself wanting to.

The conversation easily flowed, and just as I prepared to get Matthew ready for bedtime Randy indicated it was time for him to leave. Fumbling for propriety I immediately sought shelter in my routine of putting Matt to bed when my mother looked at me and gently said, "Kel, why don't you walk Randy to the car, and I'll take care of Matt?"

Picking up on my hesitation she continued, "You can say good night to him when you get back in. He won't be asleep."

Optionless. There was no way I could politely decline even if I wanted to, but the thought of not knowing what to say to him was petrifying. I was cornered with no way out and no wiggle room; I was back looking for a place to hide but knew that without Randy making a move to protest, I had no choice. I had to go to the closet, put on my coat and walk out the door he had just opened.

We walked across the parking lot in relative silence, hands in our respective pockets as my eyes remained fixed on anything but his. He leaned in to start his car then motioned me toward mine, explaining that my mom had asked him to check something on it. He popped the hood as I obligatorily stood there, wishing for words to flow like they had in the kitchen between my family and him, but I had none. Fear fought to crawl its way to the surface, beckoning me to join him back in seclusion while, like an inner battle of wills, the other voice repeated, "You're fine, just stand still."

As if being summoned by the reverie, I leapt back into the conversation when he asked me if I had been dating anyone. Taken aback by the need to be candid, I nodded my head yes then quickly added that our faiths were different, defining it as "nothing serious." The evening's darkness cloaked his reaction as he finished his repair, wiped his hands, then shut the hood and quietly said, "Well, Kelly, I'm going to do this one more time. If you'd like to go to dinner with me so we could talk… let me know when."

Then he stood there looking at me and I stood there unable to move. I looked at him, briefly, but at least I looked at him, and I knew just like I did that Saturday morning with my mother that I needed to do this. I watched my feet as they kicked at the loose pavement; something about this man was haunting to me and no matter how I tried to avoid or escape him, he was relentless in his pursuit. Although I didn't fully understand him, and trusted him even less, I knew this past week had brought me so far out of my isolated realm of existence that I couldn't go back if I wanted to. I slowly lifted my head, my hands clenched tight deep into my pockets, and quietly said, "When?"

"Well, I'm open Friday night. Does that work?" he asked.

"Yes."

"And you won't cancel on me?"

Smirking, I shook my head no. He added, "Promise?"

"Yes," I said, nodding my head.

"Okay, I'll call you Thursday and let you know when. Alright?"

I tried to grin, then nodded in agreement.

Seconds later standing on the steps I watched as he drove away, stunned by my own lack of resolve. Looking up, I watched the white steam of air leave my lungs, and said, "I don't know what You're up to, but it better be something good."

CHAPTER TWENTY-THREE

First Impressions

PACING THE FLOOR, I thought my skin was going to jump off my body as I waited for the doorbell to ring. I hated being ready early; the extra time always allowed my mind to wander into places it had no business going, which made my heart hammer, my hands sweat and my tongue stick to the roof of my mouth. I tried to occupy the idleness by coloring with Matt, but inevitably the crayon would somehow find its way outside the lines, which exasperated me even more. So instead I just watched. With a deep exhale, my jitters found their release through my shaking leg and the drumming fingers on the table. It wasn't long before my mother chided me, "Kelly, STOP it!! You're making me crazy."

No sooner did she finish her command then the sound of the doorbell filled the room, acting like a period to her statement. For seconds it felt like time stood still. I looked at her wide eyed, desperately wishing she would give me a list of things I should talk about. Instead, she just smiled, patted my hand and said, "You're going to be fine. Now go get the door."

It was mid-November and the briskness of the night air filled the room as Randy walked in to say hello. True to his nature, after our initial greeting he spoke with my mother and then directed his full attention to Matthew, discussing what he was coloring and inquiring about his evening's plans. Intrigued by the ease with which he conducted himself, my nerves began to take second place to the curiosity I felt about this man. I was completely perplexed by how anyone, especially a man, could be so genuinely kind with people on a consistent basis. Based on my prior experiences, he was an anomaly. So with an internal shake of my head I dismissed my curiosity by telling myself there had to be something wrong with him.

As Randy began to gently wrap up his conversation with my three year old, he lifted my coat, motioning me with a nod of his head that it was time to leave. He turned to say goodnight to my mother by telling her he'd have me home before 11:00 p.m. Within minutes I had been transported from my state of nervous frenzy to being a buckled in passenger heading toward an unfamiliar restaurant with a man whose presence, frankly, scared the life out of me.

Interestingly enough, while I felt like I was on "high alert" ever since I had committed to having dinner with him, the fear I felt in the car was different than the fear that previously consumed me. Although I knew I had wandered a great distance from the entrance of my cave, the land of unfamiliar no longer felt quite so unstable; it was as if the assurance he demonstrated from the moment he arrived somehow stabilized the ground underneath me, and I felt almost safe in exploring this undiscovered territory.

The evening was spent sharing dinner and, for the most part, unstrained conversation. Although my awareness of being out in the open never completely left me, there were definite moments when the conversation got too close and I would flee to find shelter until it was safe to come back out. Randy was, by some means, innately aware of those moments and had the ability to discern exactly when his questions struck too close to heart and would immediately navigate the conversation in a different direction.

Then when the awkwardness of the moment would lift, I would find myself yet again like a little girl peeking out from behind a barrier, assessing the danger before I would step entirely out from behind my wall of protection. Only when I was fully convinced the danger of complete exposure had vanished would I reengage with him and the conversation would easily flow once again. The majority of the dinner was spent as if we were dining on a teeter-totter; I was skittish then at ease then skittish, etc.

Perhaps my nerves made the evening feel like it went by entirely too fast because before I was really ready for it to end, I was watching Randy lay down his money to pay the bill. I sat still, folding my hands in my lap wondering why I was so weird when I heard him ask, "Kelly, are you about ready to go?"

Convinced my behavior had got the best of him I looked at him, shrugged one shoulder and said, "Sure, if you are."

We left the restaurant the same way we had come in: him helping me with my coat, leading me to the entrance and holding the doors for me. It wasn't until we were buckled in the car waiting for it to warm up that Randy asked if I would be interested in coming over to his house, "There's a Christian song I would love for you to hear."

I tried to hide the skepticism and distrust that immediately washed over me as I mentally questioned the intentions of this incredibly handsome man who owned his own home and was now inviting me to come over and listen to music. Experience screamed at me, "You've got to be kidding. You're really going to believe him?"

However, Present reminded me that his behavior, both now and over the past six months, warranted no serious concern. He had never done anything except be a gentleman, and besides, unlike my previous boyfriend, my mother deeply approved of this man; there were no verbal warnings lingering in my head about him.

Sensing my uncertainty, he said, "Kelly, it's okay if you don't want to. The song I wanted you to hear helped me make the decision to get baptized. I just thought you'd like it—we can do it another time."

My eyes locked on his and for the first time that night, I didn't immediately look away. Something about him was completely sincere and trustworthy so before I lost my nerve I replied, "No, no…it's okay. We can go. I'd like to hear it… really."

He responded with an easy grin then shifted his car into drive and headed toward home. Minutes into the car ride, Silence joined me in an effort to reassure my nagging doubts, and although I fought to stay calm, Fear began screaming at me, "WHAT?? What did you do?"

I leaned my head back on the headrest and let Silence speak

for me, "She'll just find a way to run out if he gets weird."

Fear quickly argued back, "Whatever...you were stupid to even agree to this." Then thick in sarcasm he continued, "Sure...it's Christian music he wants to you to hear. Really?"

The bantering in my head seemed to drown out everything else around me, leaving me no option but to look out the passenger window and become preoccupied with the inner war that was raging inside.

By the time I walked into Randy's house all that I could think of was Silence's instruction to find a way out in case things got "weird." One of the first things I noticed was a back exit through the kitchen, reassuring me that safety was just a short distance away if needed. His request to take my coat invaded my planning strategy and summoned me back into real time, making me aware that I was still shivering from the chill in the air so I declined his offer and just sat down, stiff and as closed off as humanly possible.

As he thumbed through his record collection, Randy explained the background story of why the song "Watch the Lamb" held such meaning for him. Since he hadn't grown up in the church, the concept of faith and Jesus' ministry were fairly new ideas, and this particular song helped him feel the power behind Jesus' sacrifice. I listened as he spoke with such sincerity that I didn't have the heart to tell him I had heard the song countless times before. I just smiled as if I understood, my hands deeply burrowed in the pockets of my coat, and listened as the song began.

There is a critical verse in the song when Ray Boltz brings the story to a pivotal moment and, regardless of how many times you've heard it, thousands of goose bumps inevitably cover your skin. Undoubtedly as if timing couldn't get any worse, it was right at that instant, as Randy's eyes were closed and he was consumed in worship, I was overcome with the gnawing awareness that I was going to be sick. I tried fending off the gurgling in my stomach and realized that despite shedding my coat beads of sweat were starting to roll down the sides of my head. Then as if it was a well planned, synchronized crescendo, right when Boltz sings "YOU carry His cross," I got up, ran to the bathroom, turned the faucets on full blast in hopes of disguising the noise and began heaving my guts out.

Some time later, as my head lay draped across my arm, the only sound I could hear was the flow of water coming from the faucet. The song was over and silence filled the atmosphere that was just on the other side of the door. Catching a deep breath, I took an extra second to stabilize myself, then did the best I could to repair my disheveled appearance. Making one final effort to wipe clean the smeared mascara, I turned the water off and patted my face, praying the whole time he didn't hear anything.

For a girl who doesn't like to draw attention to herself, you certainly figured out a way to do so tonight, I told myself as I stood at the door trying to find courage enough to open it. I closed my eyes, shaking my head in disbelief, realizing that despite all of my best efforts the evening had pretty much been a disaster. The sadness I felt kind of surprised me as I let the thought settle. Unsure of what else I could do, I straightened myself up one final time, turned the knob of the door and walked out, asking Randy, "Can you take me home, please?"

Being enveloped by the chill of the November air initially

made me believe that the worst part of being sick was over and that I could make it the short distance home without having to will myself not to get sick again. However, minutes into the drive I discovered that that was merely a fleeting thought and was reduced to plastering my head against the passenger window in hopes the outside temperature would help keep things where they belonged, thereby leaving me my dignity.

But the last few minutes of the drive were spent fighting the rising gurgling of my stomach. No matter how much I wanted to push it back down where it belonged, it kept trying to crawl its way up through my digestive tract. I was already convinced that he believed I was a certifiable nut case after this evening so there was no way I could verbalize my latest exploits in his bathroom, let alone ask him to pull over. I figured I would just try to play it cool and he would never have to know.

Silence had completely filled the car as Randy made his final turn onto the street where I lived. While I hated to see the evening end this way, I knew I needed to get in my house before Vesuvius started erupting again. Wishing he would drive faster, I quietly mapped out my strategy: I wouldn't wait for him to open my door, I would get out as soon as he parked the car, then I would walk brusquely, but not so fast that it would be rude, to my door, thank him for dinner and say goodnight. He'd never know and maybe I could salvage some of the evening.

Everything went according to plan, except my underestimation of his gentleman quality. Randy wasn't exactly comfortable with my expedient exit from the automobile, and while he kept pace with me all the way to the door, he began to linger in saying goodbye. For some unexplainable reason I heard him say, "Kelly, I had a nice time tonight. I enjoyed you."

The first thing I thought was, *Are you kidding me? You really had a nice time?* But afraid of what the somersault in my stomach would do if given an opportunity to act, I just quickly grinned and said, "Thank you, me too," groping for the doorknob. When I turned back to him, those eyes of his began their piercing stare and I was frozen still in place. *No, I thought to myself, he wants to kiss me and he doesn't know. How am I supposed to kiss him when that vile taste has taken residence in my mouth?*

How a hundred questions can go through one's brain in a second or two is incomprehensible to me, but they did. And before I knew it, he was leaning down and all I could do was permanently seal my mouth together and not move. Apprehension, protection, and embarrassment coursed through my mind all at once; focusing on the moment was pointless. All I could think was to do everything possible to prevent discovery. I never thought about the message my lack of response was sending; I just figured it would go down as the worst kiss on record ... ever.

Randy, none the wiser about my earlier bathroom escapades, stepped back and cautiously smiled one last time. Then he opened the door for me and said goodnight. I watched him for just a second as he got into his car, then I closed the door. There was something about that man that I found completely fascinating. I closed my eyes and tried to extract the sweetness out of the evening, and while the kiss may have not sealed the deal, it had certainly got my attention.

CHAPTER TWENTY-FOUR

Steps of Faith

THE FOLLOWING SUNDAY evening my mother invited Randy
over after church for another cup of cocoa; it seemed to be
the beverage of choice where he was concerned. I retreated
to my inner silence and quietly observed him, trying to figure
out why he chose to return, especially after my erratic Friday
night behavior. Baffled by his tenacity I lost myself in toddler
activities, hoping to avoid any and all future loss of dignity
and vulnerability. Meanwhile, he seemed quite content in
occupying himself in conversation with my mother.

I found a reprieve from my inner hiding place as Matthew's
bedtime approached. Deciding to take advantage of my own
personal escape route, I helped Matthew prematurely clean up
his things and ushered him upstairs. Now free from Randy's
persistent penetrating eyes, I could slowly exhale as I climbed
the stairs toward Matt's bedroom. It wasn't until I noticed
the lull in conversation quickly being replaced with hushed

whispers that my ears dialed in like radar.

"Carol, I'm not sure how well Friday night went," was Randy's first audible comment.

"Hmmm, I'm surprised. She said she had a good time," replied my mother.

Straining to hear, I pulled Matthew on my lap as I sat on the top step and quietly motioned him to shhh, praying he didn't ask his all too familiar question, "Why Mommy? Why do we have to shhh?"

Thankfully, he interpreted the moment as an opportunity to be held, threw his arms around my neck and sat still. Their conversation continued when Randy sounded as surprised as his question, "Really?... She had a good time? I'm surprised."

"Why?...Didn't you?"

I held my breath feeling Fear surface, *What if he says no? Then what? Now you like the guy and if he says no, you're right back where you started. Then what are you going to do? Stupid, you shouldn't have even gone.*

"Yeah, I had a great time, but I don't think she did." Randy added, "She didn't act like it anyway."

I felt the tension ease as I slowly exhaled and Matthew snuggled closer. Afraid of discovery, I sat frozen in place too intrigued by their conversation to move, not wanting to miss anything. But in those seconds of self awareness my mother must have asked what I did, because the next thing I heard was Randy's explanation of what happened at his house while we listened to the song, and then he jumped right to the part when I asked him to take me home.

Silence consumed the air in the kitchen and I knew that while I couldn't actually see her silently encouraging him to continue, the look on my mother's face would have said it all. I leaned forward to hear better when the sound of Randy clearing his throat rolled up the stairs. "Well," he paused, "when I tried to kiss her goodnight, it was like kissing a wall. She didn't seem the least bit interested."

Sitting on that top step, it took everything I had not to laugh out loud. The combination of not wanting to be noticed and Matthew asleep on my shoulder held my silence as I closed my eyes and like a movie replayed that awkward scene in my mind. *If only he knew what I had spared him of,* I thought.

Laughter bounded up the stairs as my mother lost herself in the miscommunication. "Oh Randy," she said, "it's not disinterest at all. Didn't she tell you what happened?"

"No, what?" he replied.

The satisfaction of knowing not all was lost was shattered as my inner voice screamed, *NOOO—oh my gosh, Mom, don't tell him. For all that's good and holy, please don't tell him.* But we failed to communicate through mental telepathy so my mother proceeded to candidly explain that I had thrown up not only in his bathroom, but had to fight getting sick all the way home.

Before she even finished her last word, my head gradually rolled back as if I had been knocked out and my eyes squeezed shut as I nearly melted from embarrassment. "Aw, Mom, you wouldn't…you didn't," I whispered to myself, secretly vowing to hit her the next time we were alone.

With his trademark tenderness shrouding his voice, Randy responded, "Really? Why didn't she tell me?"

My head lifted back up as I wondered, *What is it about this guy and how nice he is? I just don't get him.*

In a final response my mother answered, "She was too embarrassed ... but she really did have a good time."

That was enough for me. My secret was out in the open, and the one man who was more collected and proper than any person I had ever met knew the real reason behind my becoming a disheveled mess on that grand night of my opening debut. I had no clue how to proceed so instead I just stood up as quietly as possible with the weight of my sleeping son on my shoulder and tiptoed him into bed. Kneeling down to stroke his hair I thanked God for him, then asked the Lord to bless him and keep him as only He could, kissed his forehead and quietly said goodnight.

Leaning against Matthew's door jamb, I straddled between two worlds: the predictable one I had created over the past three years that was safe and routine, and the one that waited for me downstairs—the one that included a man whose presence had unknowingly and continually made me want to come further and further away from my self-induced seclusion just by his kindness. *How do these two worlds blend together?* I wondered.

I glanced over at Matthew sleeping. I was barely 21 and had already made a silent vow of protection, not only to me but to him as well. Any potential agreement to enlarge my world didn't just involve me anymore; his little life was at stake too. Caught in my own confusion, the memory of the last time I was so conflicted rushed over me, and I was instantly transported back to Ohio to the church parking lot on that snowy February night. It seemed like a lifetime had passed since then. I could feel myself back at the feet of Jesus, convinced that I didn't have the courage to accomplish the task at hand, the same way I felt at that current moment. I closed my eyes and barely tilting my head upward, whispered, "I don't know if I can do this again. I'm so frightened; I can't say goodbye twice, Lord."

And I stood there, unmoving and still. Face to face with the rawness of my fear, I realized that for the first time in a long time I wasn't being paralyzed by it. Instead, in the midst of its presence, just like that late winter night when I was 17, Peace had mysteriously entered the atmosphere and like a welcome visitor to my soul, I heard Him say, "*My daughter, I will work all things together for your good. Just trust Me.*"

CHAPTER TWENTY-FiVE

Amore

COMMITTING TO SEE Randy on a consistent basis over the next few months felt as natural as being pregnant once I had chosen life. With little effort, our relationship just evolved and grew as we gradually spent time together. Through numerous conversations we discovered we were united in thought and spirit on just about everything including faith, parenting, loss, even our physical relationship.

Undoubtedly the residual heartache from my prior experience still haunted me, which only served to reestablish my commitment to purity while Randy's pledge came from an innate sense of holiness and obedience to his faith. It was the first time I actually witnessed someone make a commitment out of a reverence for the God he served rather than for what it could or could not get him. I was admittedly amazed and often wondered if there was anything that wasn't impressive about this man.

It took shy of four months before we both knew that marriage was inevitable; after all, they (whoever they are) say, "When you know, you know," and it didn't take long for us to *know*. I knew I enjoyed his company, and there was something about his gentle manner that seemed to penetrate most of my defenses. And although there was still a sizable amount of my heart that remained back in Ohio, the part that had come to terms with living in Indiana knew that I loved him. Perhaps one could say that I loved him with everything I had at the moment; the rest of me was still scattered and strewn across a valley in northeast Ohio.

By early March my mother had purchased a home just across the street from where Randy lived, which allowed for all of us to incorporate a workable routine into our daily lives. Running back and forth between the two houses quickly became commonplace, so it was of no particular interest to me when my mother offered to keep Matthew so I could go see Randy after work one day.

Greeting me at the door, Randy appeared collected and polished despite his loosened tie and unbuttoned collar. He had his mail in one hand and had obviously just started to skim through it when I arrived but instead invited me to sit down as he laid it on the table. I watched him as he walked back over and joined me on the couch, and for as much as Silence used to befriend and consume my time, Chatter had replaced him and decided to emerge because I started to rattle on about my day, Matt's day, what was for dinner and the evening's plans... anything that would fill the space between us until finally Randy looked at me and quietly said, "Kelly, I need you to be quiet for a minute."

My mind stopped dead in its tracks as if it had been suddenly derailed, and I fought to not be irritated by his apparent lack of interest in my ramblings. I blinked twice at him then said, "Oh...well, okay then."

In a way completely uncharacteristic to him he began to squirm and fidget, and I couldn't help but wonder what was wrong with him. He started biting his lip and looking around as if he was waiting for the words to appear in the air. When he leaned over to stand up, countless negative thoughts began to assault my confidence until, taking one step closer to me, he slowly knelt down on one knee and said, "Kelly..."

Those negative thoughts instantly turned into what felt like one hundred questions like, *Is he really?* ...Which got answered with, *This is it.* Then the biggest one yet... *Am I really ready for this?*

Praying that my face didn't betray my thoughts, I looked at him until his gaze became too intense and I had to look down. "Kelly...will you marry me?"

I looked up ever so slightly terrified by the intensity of the emotion, but knew that I had to see him. I beheld the magnitude of emotion in his eyes for as long as I could before I looked down at the open box lying in the palm of his hand. Briefly I glanced back up at him as I tried to absorb all that was happening, then had to look back down. That's when he began to explain. "I spoke with your mom before I did this, and she shared with me that she had saved the diamonds your dad gave to her. You need to know the middle stone on the engagement ring is the one he gave your mom when he asked her to marry him." Then he paused, "I thought you would like it more than anything I could buy."

For as much as Chatter had walked in the house with me, Silence had somehow taken her place. I was dumbfounded by his kindness and sensitivity, not only to our relationship but to the unspoken need I had to be connected to my father. Minutes passed as I tried to process everything that had gone into Randy's offer, when suddenly I realized in the midst of so much vulnerability Fear was nowhere to be found. There I sat completely emotionally exposed, and something that had been such an integral part of my life for so long failed to surface at the expected time. Without Fear I wasn't exactly sure how I felt so for a split second I didn't feel anything other than complete certainty that I needed to do this…no…I *wanted* to do this.

Like rolling waves the evolution of our relationship washed over me, and the longer I sat there, the more my confidence grew in what I was about to commit to. I knew that this man, who had more honor and integrity than anyone I had ever met, wanted to be with me and that was enough, solely enough for me to say, "Yes."

Randy and I spoke at length that evening about how we felt and if we knew exactly what we were getting into by creating an immediate family. We discussed his heart for Matthew and what it would mean to accept the ensuing responsibility of being his father, which led to where I was emotionally with everything that had happened in Ohio. I desperately wanted to dismiss the emotional havoc the memories plagued me with and tried to skirt the issue by avoiding the conversation. I wasn't willing to go back in the pit; I had become quite comfortable living out in the open where the air was fresh and light abounded.

"Well," Randy said, holding my hand, "Here's the thing."

"What?" I inquired.

"I love you, Kelly, and want to marry you. However…" he stopped.

I closed my eyes sensing he was going to require something of me I wasn't sure I could give him. The seconds ticked off the clock that sat on the desk as I mentally tried to find an escape route from the very moment that was confronting me. My eyes, blurred by tears brought on by a rediscovered force of terror, lifted to look at him.

He continued, "However, I won't marry you unless you do one thing. I want you to go to counseling; you need the help, Kelly."

I pulled my hands away from his clasp and wiped my eyes. I fought against the indignation that wanted to resist and hurl insults at him—anything to avoid having to go back. But in the end I knew he was right; whatever it was that was tormenting me I couldn't seem to get rid of on my own, and it had already taken so much from me. Jesus' words instantly came back to me, "*The thief does not come except to steal, and to kill, and to destroy. I have come that they may have life, and that they may have it more abundantly*" (John 10:10).

Something about Randy's offer represented new life, but sitting there on that couch I knew I had to decide. Would I reach out and grab it or choose to remain hidden because Fear would keep me from reentering that cave to retrieve whatever I had left behind? I shifted my eyes toward the floor and thought about the last four months, then thought about life by myself. I knew without question there was no comparison. Then, like a flood, Matthew's sweet face and the impact my decision would have on him filled my mind's eye and that's when I knew the answer. I didn't want his life or his future jeopardized because Fear was trying to prevent me from choosing mine.

I closed my eyes as I drew in a deep inhale and silently begged the Lord for the courage it would take to persevere, then cautiously looked up at Randy and said, "Okay....Yes, I'll go to counseling." He smiled as he leaned in to kiss me. Seconds later I continued, "I don't know who and I don't know where, but I'll get the help I need...I promise."

CHAPTER TWENTY-SIX

Taking Back the Ground

IT DIDN'T TAKE long before my weekly counseling sessions began. As with most things, if I had known what I was really signing up for I probably would not have committed to go. On some level I was faintly aware that my heart was not fully intact, but to what extent I would have to journey backward to retrieve its pieces was admittedly unclear to me.

Time had somehow scabbed over the effects of the past three or four years, and somewhere along the way I had ceased walking around as if I had a cavern for a heart. What I didn't understand was that the life I had been building was standing on a thin veneer of existence and that the cavern lay broad and wide just below the foundation; any crack or shift in the fault line could easily give way and fall into the unseen sinkhole underneath.

The first time I walked into the counselor's office I was

fully prepared to familiarize him with the loss of my father, my childhood, and the back and forth tug of war I lived the last years of high school. I figured those were the real source of my issues and yet, while he patiently listened and asked some probing questions, he never really delved into any of them. Rather, as our weekly meetings continued he became like a magnet drawn to the more recent issues at hand and relentlessly pursued my prior relationship with a married man, the dual pregnancies and my inability to completely break free from the emotional hold it continued to have on me.

No matter what questions he asked or what explanations he gave, I countered his arguments by describing that relationship as loyal and sacred. I failed to see it the same as everyone else. Instead, I found it honorable that he returned to his wife, and I had convinced myself that what we had shared was real and that in another time or place it would have worked. The idea that he may have used or taken advantage of me had never crossed my mind.

After nearly three months of weekly sessions and various different attempted approaches at the truth, my counselor asked if he could share a particular passage of Scripture with me, explaining that I might relate to the young girl in the story. After a quick verbal assent, he began:

> After this Absalom the son of David had a lovely sister, whose name was Tamar; and Amnon the son of David loved her. Amnon was so distressed over his sister Tamar that he became sick; for she was a virgin. And it was improper for Amnon to do anything to her. But Amnon had a friend whose name was Jonadab the son of Shimeah, David's brother. Now Jonadab was a very crafty

man. And he said to him, "Why are you, the king's son, becoming thinner day after day? Will you not tell me?" Amnon said to him, "I love Tamar, my brother Absalom's sister." So Jonadab said to him, "Lie down on your bed and pretend to be ill. And when your father comes to see you, say to him, 'Please let my sister Tamar come and give me food, and prepare the food in my sight, that I may see it and eat it from her hand.'" Then Amnon lay down and pretended to be ill; and when the king came to see him, Amnon said to the king, "Please let Tamar my sister come and make a couple of cakes for me in my sight, that I may eat from her hand." And David sent home to Tamar, saying, "Now go to your brother Amnon's house, and prepare food for him."

So Tamar went to her brother Amnon's house, and he was lying down. Then she took flour and kneaded it, made cakes in his sight, and baked the cakes. And she took the pan and placed them out before him, but he refused to eat. Then Amnon said, "Have everyone go out from me." And they all went out from him. Then Amnon said to Tamar, "Bring the food into the bedroom that I may eat from your hand." And Tamar took the cakes which she had made, and brought them to Amnon her brother in the bedroom. Now when she had brought them to him to eat, he took hold of her and said to her, "Come, lie with me, my sister." But she answered him, "No, my brother, do not force me, for no such thing should be done in Israel. Do not do this disgraceful thing! And I, where could I take my shame? And as for you, you would be like one of the fools in Israel. Now therefore, please speak to the king, for he will not withhold me from you." However, he would not heed her voice, and being stronger than she, he forced her and lay with her.

Then Amnon hated her exceedingly, so that the hatred with which he hated her was greater than the love with which he had loved her. And Amnon said to her, "Arise, be gone!" So she said to him, "No, indeed! This evil of sending me away is worse than the other that you did to me." But he would not listen to her. Then he called his servant who attended him, and said, "Here! Put this woman out, away from me, and bolt the door behind her." Now she had on a robe of many colors, for the king's virgin daughters wore such apparel. And his servant put her out and bolted the door behind her. Then Tamar put ashes on her head, and tore her robe of many colors that was on her, and laid her hand on her head and went away crying bitterly. (2 Samuel 13:6-19)

He slowly closed his Bible and let the story sink in while I sat there, lost for words, trying desperately to organize my thoughts. *What am I supposed to make of that?* I wondered.

"I don't know what to say," I told him.

"Kelly," he asked, "what stands out from that story?"

"She was thrown out—left after she had been with him," I quietly responded.

"Okay. How is your story different?" he asked.

"He forced her. I wasn't forced."

"No, you weren't," he agreed, nodding his head.

Silence filled the room and I felt Tamar's experience become real in my spirit. There was something about her story that seemed to deeply resonate with me but I didn't understand why. I asked, "Why do I feel like her? Like Tamar? I wasn't raped."

"Because Kelly, Amnon didn't just rape Tamar physically," he paused. "He raped her emotionally. Listen to Amnon's motives again:

> "Then Amnon lay down and pretended to be ill; and when the king came to see him, Amnon said to the king, 'Please let Tamar my sister come and make a couple of cakes for me in my sight, that I may eat from her hand.'"

He continued, "You feel like her because, though you weren't physically raped, you were emotionally raped just like Tamar. He manipulated and took advantage of your circumstances, then once he had his way and things got too complicated, just like Tamar, he put you out. Until you allow God to heal you of that, your heart will remain in pieces."

The mood in the room was somber and I felt as if I had been sucker punched and the wind had been knocked out of me. I didn't want to believe him, yet somewhere way below the surface I knew that what he spoke was truth. I felt Silence surface as my mind rehashed an earlier conversation with my mother: "Kelly, you need to think twice before you file for paternity. If he won't help you out of a place of love, do you really think a law will change his heart?"

Somehow, despite the pain that was seeping through the scab, I began to consider that maybe his heart was never there in the first place; perhaps, whether in whole or in part, there was some semblance of truth in what I was hearing. I shut my eyes, wishing I could go back to the early days when I was carefree and our relationship was just fun, nothing else. No weight, nothing physical—just playfulness and ease; that's when I was the happiest. *How did things get so complicated?*

I wondered.

I leaned forward in my chair, numb but aware I was no longer able to find refuge in my own created sense of reality. The truth was I had believed in something that never truly existed; just like Amnon lured his sister pretending to be sick, he had lured me under his own false pretenses and in the end we were both thrown out.

The truth behind that reality slowly illuminated my once inhabited cave as if someone had ordered the stage lights to be brought up, and for the first time since that New Year's Eve when he told me he was going back to his wife, I had a sudden desire to move forward. Desperate to put things behind me, I penetrated the silence by asking, "So now what?"

"Well, Kelly, let me explain something first. Our society is centered on ceremonial markers. For example, when a person graduates, he or she goes through a graduation ceremony, or when two people get married, there's a wedding. Does that make sense?"

I silently nodded, wondering what this had to do with anything.

"Well," he continued, "I think some of the trouble lies in the fact that you have never gone through your own 'separation ceremony.'"

Looking at him quizzically, my eyes conveyed my confusion.

"Did he ever give you anything? Jewelry? Presents? Anything?" he asked.

I thought about our last Christmas together—the one before he went back to his wife. The one before I got pregnant—our first one. Glimpses of our gift exchange flashed through my mind as I reflected on how much he loved what I bought him, then mentally reopened the two gifts that I still cherished. Hesitantly I said "Yes," not sure where he was going with this.

"Can you tell me what they are?"

Skeptical of his intentions I said, "A jacket," then stopped.

"And?" the counselor pressed.

I reminisced on how he had me carry the other present, convincing me it was for someone else, then I said, "A jewelry box."

"Okay, good. Those things symbolize something to you, don't they?"

Wondering if he would ever quit I felt my throat tighten and, despite my resistance, my eyes filled with tears as I silently nodded my head in agreement.

"It was never your choice to say goodbye, was it?" he asked.

I shook my head no.

"There's a good part of you that still hasn't let go of that relationship, Kelly. So here's what I'd like you to do, and I'm not going to say this will be easy, because it's not. It's going to hurt like hell. But if you want healing, this is your first step."

"Just tell me," I said, never wanting anything over with so badly in all my life.

He explained, "I'd like you to take those two gifts you mentioned and give them away."

My mind went on audible auto response, "What?... Why?... NO, I don't want to."

"I know you don't, but in giving them away you will be taking the first steps toward saying your own goodbye. This is the only way that you can go back and reclaim some of your heart. It's your choice, Kelly."

The disbelief I felt followed me through the parking lot, into my car and all the way back to Randy's house as I shared with him about the day's session.

"Why?" I asked Randy, "Why would he want me to do this? It's not like I can give Matthew away, and he came from him."

Randy just sat and looked at me with his eyes full of compassion and mercy, and said, "I'm sorry. I know this is hard."

"If I give them away, who do I give them to?" I asked, "Just anybody?" desperately hoping that I had found a viable argument to keep them. I continued, "They're really nice things. I can't give them to just anybody."

"I don't know, Kel, I'm sure God will show you somebody."

I closed my eyes, convinced that the God I knew would not require anything to hurt quite so much. "I just don't understand, why do I have to do this?" I asked for the umpteenth time.

With a single question in response, Randy put the whole thing into perspective, "I guess the bigger question is, Kelly, why you *wouldn't* want to."

Like a stake driven right to the heart his question, cloaked in such grace, penetrated my confusion just like my mother's words from two years ago spoke through the blackness that had enveloped my soul. Truth again had found its rightful place in the midst of such torment, and I knew that if I wanted any chance of full recovery I had to walk this task out.

Silently vowing to cooperate first, I then looked at Randy and said, "Okay, I'll do it. I don't know to whom, but I'll give them away."

He held my hands, leaned his forehead on mine and said, "I know this isn't easy, but you're doing it. It'll be worth it in the end."

Just above a whisper I agreed, "I know. Thank you."

"For what? I didn't do anything."

"You're here, walking it out right next to me."

"We'll get there, Kel, one step at a time. It's how Jesus got through the cross, one step at a time."

Then we just sat there—quiet, in the moment—not fully understanding how far back we would have to go to retrieve what had been lost but committed, no matter what, to do it together.

CHAPTER TWENTY-SEVEN

Acts of Obedience

SO MANY OF the steps I took during the days following the Tamar counseling session were pure blind acts of obedience. I never fully understood what really lay on the other side of the counselor's requirement; I just knew the people I had come to trust the most were all directing me down the same path so clearly it made sense for me to listen. It wasn't as if I could consciously declare, "Oh, this is what God is telling me to do, so I'll do it." It was more like I was blindfolded and the only way to reach my goal was to listen to the familiar voices pointing me in the right direction. I couldn't tangibly see where I was headed; I just trusted that by giving my things away it would somehow help me get there, wherever that was.

The Sunday following my counseling appointment, while I was at church, I sat with my mother as she spoke with an elderly woman named Betty who had just recently lost her husband. Betty was a portly woman with gray hair, immaculately dressed in her yellow suit and everything she wore was very coordinated, including hand bag, jewelry and shoes. I thought her to be extremely well decorated without appearing gawdy or cheap.

As normal, I sat as a silent participant in the conversation and listened as Betty spoke of her 50-plus year marriage and how much she missed her life's partner. I couldn't help but notice that despite her grief, she had been meticulous in her efforts to make herself presentable and the strength of her spirit seemed to be her final accessory.

I was intrigued by her story, captivated by the thought of how one faces daily life without her life's partner when I fought to face life after loving someone for only a year or so. Her strength astounded me, and the more she spoke, the more intently I chose to listen. She shared the story of how the two had met, showed us pictures of their children, and shared the history they had created. Then she explained how each piece of jewelry she wore symbolized a particular aspect of their relationship: her wedding ring was her original ring from the '30s... she never wanted it replaced. A bracelet was for an anniversary, and her earrings were a birthday present. It was as if each piece, if it could talk, would tell its own story. I found myself wanting so badly to listen... something about their longevity and stability was overwhelmingly appealing.

I looked down at my own engagement ring and wondered how long it would take before it would represent a part of my own story with Randy. I marveled, realizing that in the few weeks that I had worn it, it had already come to symbolize so much, making it all the more valuable to me. It was something I knew I would always safeguard...that's when I knew she was the one—she was the person who was supposed to have the jewelry box. *Strange,* I thought, *meeting her today of all days.* I tried to dismiss the thought and refocus on her story, but whatever was urging me to present the idea kept getting stronger and stronger until it was impossible to ignore. I waited, almost hoping for my apprehension to surface, something to make me think twice about what I was about to do, but Silence was the only thing I could find. I fought to stay quiet, hoping I could just talk with him, but before I knew it out came "Uh, excuse me...Betty."

She immediately quit talking and turned her head toward me, followed by my mother.

"Uh...," I looked down, watching my thumb and index finger twist my ring, "I'm sorry to interrupt, but I need to ask you something."

She sat up a bit straighter and kindly asked, "What is it?"

"Well...," I felt my throat start its all too familiar constriction. "Well, I have this jewelry box and it's really nice.....and, well, I...I need to give it to you." *So much for asking,* I thought.

Clearly confused, she said, "Well, I don't understand," looking at my mother for clarity.

Embarrassed by my obvious emotional state, all I could say was, "I know...it doesn't make any sense to you, but I really need to do this."

With uncertainty plaguing her voice, all she could say was, "Well...okay," with a half statement, half question sound.

I quickly exhaled, wondering why I just did that. "Thank you," I said, leaning back in my chair. "I'd like to bring it by tonight if that's okay."

And, at that, we exchanged phone numbers and her address so I could bring it by later that evening.

It was nearly dusk when I gently placed the jewelry box in my back seat and tossed the jacket next to it. I turned, unsure exactly how I was going to get through this, and looked to my mom. "You can do this," she said as she hugged me before I got in the car, "I know you can."

Betty's house was nearly 20 minutes away, and thankfully the car somehow went on autopilot so my mind could travel down memory lane relatively uninterrupted. This time, however, the journey didn't begin at Christmas like it had in the counselor's office. It started all the way back to the first day I met him. I could still see us standing in the middle of the store as if the scene had been permanently seared into my memory, his comments about my necklace replaying in my ears. Then, my mother's admonition struck me again without warning and continued to hover like a cloud over my mental journey.

The next stop was his first phone call requesting a date, and my polite decline because I needed a job. I found myself wondering if that was when he became like Amnon "pretending to be sick." *Had his manipulation started even then?* I tried to dismiss the thought as quickly as it surfaced. *Certainly he cared,"* I told myself, *why else would he have stuck around for so long?*

My rationalizing continued, *I couldn't have been that blind.* I shook my head in disbelief—at whom or what I didn't know. Him? Me? Both?

I thought about the early days of waking up and being thankful I hadn't gone too far physically with him. It hadn't been so long that I couldn't remember the place when I was still whole and intact. Turning a corner, I asked myself for the thousandth time, *Why didn't you listen?*

Memories of school and the place in the park where he always knew to find me took me further through my past. I thought about how I had always believed he had been there for me when no one else was, how easy he was to talk with, and for the first time in three years, I realized it was his friendship that I missed the most.

Noting the corresponding address, I made the right-hand turn into Betty's driveway, listening as the car's tires crunched across the gravel. Pulling forward, my headlights illuminated the little house that once had been shiny and new with white siding but now was discolored by weather and age. One light was on in the window to the left of the door, and the green hued shadows from the TV danced through the open curtain, giving a Northern Lights effect to the space just outside the window. I turned the key toward me and listened to the dying hum of the engine and then just sat there. Perhaps unbeknownst to me, I figured if I didn't move I really wouldn't have to say goodbye. Leaning my head on the headrest, I closed my eyes and let every facet of our relationship walk, skip or run through my mind one last time. Like Betty's treasured symbols of relational victory, I prayed my memories would stay safe in that jewelry box—they were all I had left.

With a deep inhale, my fingers fumbled their way to the door handle and before I changed my mind, I pulled open the door. *This is it*, I told myself. *You can do this.*

I took the necessary two steps, grabbed the handle and opened the back door. I stood there staring at that box and let the awareness wash over me that it had come to represent so much more than just a jewelry holder. *How do I do this?* I questioned. *How do I actually let go?*

It took just a few moments before I began to understand that it didn't matter what or how my mother or Randy or anyone else defined my relationship with him. I couldn't believe something just because they did; what really mattered was what I believed the relationship was. That's when I knew that what I was about to do, the reality behind this simple solitary act, would mark the death of that core belief. For the first time I innately *knew* that it wasn't just him I was letting go of when I relinquished that jewelry box—it was everything I believed we would be and do together. It was the death of the existence I had spent years dreaming about.

I don't know how long I stood there—long enough for me to marinate on the truth, then realize time was of the essence. *It's never going to get any easier*, I whispered.

As I walked toward Betty's front door, I squeezed that jewelry box as if it alone held all that mattered to me. The difficult process of letting go that the counselor spoke of was becoming more real to me by the second, and I knew that when I handed that box over to Betty a piece of me would go with it. I quickly rapped on the door three times before I changed my mind, then tried to maintain composure as she opened the door.

"Well, hi, honey," Betty said.

"Hi," I half smiled. Wanting to get it over with, I immediately began moving the box toward her, "Well, here it is."

"Honey, don't you want to come in first?" she asked,

moving to the side of the doorframe.

Taking three short sequential gasps for air I stammered, "Nnno...no, thank you. I really need to get going," handing her the box.

"Why, thank you," her voice conveyed her bewilderment.

I hesitated, unable to make myself move, then closed my eyes and nodded a silent "you're welcome." I quickly turned, hemming off any opportunity to change my mind, and slowly walked down the three steps. The time it took to walk back to my car moved as if in slow motion and intermittently stuck on pause. Somewhere along the path Silence joined me, and although he never required me to explain, he somehow understood that I was trying to come to terms with just how much it hurt to have one's hands pried open enough to be able to finally let go.

I turned the key part way, then just sat there—no sobs, no running motor, no radio. Just Silence and my thoughts to keep me company. It's funny how five minutes of silence can feel like a lifetime.

Eventually I turned the key the rest of the way and heard the purr of the motor signify it was time to go. I sat there idling, wondering exactly where I was going, then allowed the new sense of purpose to motivate me. *One more*, I told myself, *one more.*

For the second time that evening I pushed my foot down on the brake pedal, put the car in reverse and backed out of the driveway. Although I had no concrete idea where or who to give the jacket to, I knew I had to finish what I started. I felt the gears click twice as the car went into drive, but before I headed on the familiar route back toward home, I began to ponder my options:

Friends? I didn't really have many my age that were my size, so no.

Family? No one would want it; besides I didn't want to see anyone wearing it.

Anyone needy? No one specific, but I'm open.

I had just finished my silent assessment when I passed a little strip mall on the way home and noticed a semi-trailer that had "Clothes for the Needy" painted across its side. *Unbelievable,* I thought but before I could think twice, I quickly made a left-hand turn, pulled the car around the back of the semi, and parked between the two yellow lines. *This is happening much faster than I anticipated,* I told myself. *I'm not sure what I expected, but it wasn't really this.*

Pulling the rear view mirror downward I double checked my red rimmed, puffy eyes and took a deep breath. Admittedly the jacket held less symbolism than the jewelry box and I knew it wouldn't be easy, but what threw me was where it was going. "Here, Lord? Really?" Silence responded. "A semi-truck?" Still no answer, which I've since come to understand usually means yes when He's already shown you what to do.

"Alright," I reluctantly agreed, wishing there was another way.

By the time I mustered up enough nerve to go to the worker standing by the semi, it was a fairly quick handoff. There was a moment, however, when for a split second I held the coat a bit too tightly for a bit too long, until the worker finally looked at me and inquired, "Are you sure about this?"

Like a call to obedience, I immediately let go and said, "Uh…sorry. Sure…sure. It's okay." Then, putting my head down, I turned to walk back to my car.

It wasn't until I drove away that my previous questions were finally answered. As I looked in my rearview mirror and reread the painted "Clothes for the Needy" sign, I knew while the jewelry box symbolized what I believed the relationship to be, the jacket had actually represented me. Tamar's story flooded my mind and instantly I knew that not only was I just like her, I was also just like the jacket—used, discarded and ultimately thrown out to an unknown destination.

I snickered at the cruelty of it all. *How did I get here?* I wondered, and shook my head. I thought about him, his family, and his life in Ohio and wondered if he ever thought about Matthew and me. *Did Amnon ever think about Tamar? How does a man just walk away?*

I didn't understand.

I stared at the red light and thought about where I was headed, both literally and figuratively. I thought about Randy and wondered why he stayed with me. *Does he even know what he's signing up for?* I questioned, but I had no answers. I had no emotion. I was spent, like a rag doll—limp and without resistance.

I drove home just like I had driven away, on autopilot, and without thinking pulled my car back into the driveway. Bracing myself for an onslaught of questions, I crossed the street and quietly tapped on Randy's door. The sound of crashing Lincoln Logs filled the room as I said, "Hey, how's it going?"

"Mommy!!" Matthew squealed in delight, running to greet me.

Squatting down to hold him, I said, "Hey, bud, how you doing?" As if he were my own personal life source, feeling his little boy arms around my neck brought some unexplainable empowerment to my soul. I knelt there, closed my eyes and savored the sweetness of his spirit. *Oh, how I miss the days when things were free and innocent,* I thought to myself.

Through closed lids, the variance of light revealed Randy's nearness. "Hey, Kel, how you doing?"

I gave no response. I couldn't—the pain, still too new, was constricting my throat like a noose around my neck. Instead I just stayed there, knelt down sandwiched between my past and my future. I thought about the mystery that surrounded God's economy, and how by giving things away I would ultimately be retrieving what rightfully belonged to me. "Lord, please let this work; please put me back together," I prayed. Then silence enveloped the three of us and though my heart still ached, it wasn't long before I recognized that this pain was different than what had previously consumed me; this ache was wrapped in the promise that while *"weeping may endure for a night, joy comes in the morning"* (Psalm 30:5).

CHAPTER TWENTY-EIGHT

The Measure of a Man

THE FIRST OF December was rapidly approaching, bringing with it our impending wedding date. Over the course of the last few months, even though I had grown considerably close to Randy I certainly had intermittent moments of questioning the lifetime commitment I was about to make. Old memories of my last "love" would sporadically taunt me, causing me to frequently play the second guessing or "what if" game. But, as usual, my mother remained steadfast and faithful to reassure me and validate Randy's character, thus helping guide me through the onslaught of fear and doubt.

During one of those "what if" moments as I wrestled with the Lord over the logic of my decision, I sensed Him ask, *"Kelly, if you had to make a list of the qualities that mattered to you in a man, what would you choose?"*

Admittedly, while my emotional experience was well beyond my chronological age of 22, some of my mentality still desperately lagged behind and I quickly responded, "Well, he'd be good looking… physically attractive… and he'd be fun to be around."

The Lord continued, *"Okay…what do you need the most in your life?"*

I knew the answer immediately. The shame and regret I held over the choices I had made in Ohio still haunted me like a stain on my soul I couldn't get clean. So I told the Lord, "Your grace and mercy."

Seconds passed, leaving me uncertain as to exactly how all the pieces fit together. I tried to understand why the Lord would ask me about what I needed when I had come to Him seeking insight about getting married. "How does all this fit together, Lord?" I sat silent trying to make sense of it all when I felt the Lord say, *"Randy is those very things you just asked for. You see, Kelly, I knew what you needed before you even asked for it. Because he abides in grace and mercy, I will use the very essence of his character to bring about your healing."*

I sat stunned, floored by the reality that the God of all creation cared enough or even knew me enough to see past my sin right into the heart of my need. Then thoughts of the past ten months began to replay across my mind as I absorbed the truth about Randy's character: his ongoing tenacity despite my rude behavior, the kindness he had continually demonstrated not just to me but to my entire family, his love for Matthew, and his unwavering support throughout the counseling. *This has to be the Lord*, I thought as I measured my emotional growth since having met Randy. *There's already been so much healing.*

I need to know, Lord. I need to know this is You. I reached for my Bible and began to search the Scriptures for confirmation. I needed to find the essence of Randy's character within the Word, and in minutes, I recorded the following:

"The discretion of a man makes him slow to anger, and his glory is to overlook a transgression." Proverbs 19:11

"He who follows righteousness and mercy finds life, righteousness and honor." Proverbs 21:21

"He who loves purity of heart and has grace on his lips, the king will be his friend." Proverbs 22:11

"Better is the poor who walks in his integrity than one perverse in his ways though he be rich."
Proverbs 28:6

I read them and reread them. And with each review of the verses, I felt the Lord write their collective truth deeper on my heart until my spirit saw the depth of Randy's character emerge on those pages. Then I began to gradually absorb that, despite my own nagging fears and hesitations, God had already begun to fulfill His promise to work all things together for my good and He was using Randy's character to do it.

I tried to let this new revelation sink deep into my soul and savor the peace that came through what I had just read. I leaned back on my bed and looked at the verses one last time. I thought about how Fear still lurked in some of the remaining undiscovered shadows of my former existence, but decided that for now he would remain there. Instead I would stay focused on what the Lord had just shown me and admit that—with as much of my heart that was intact—marrying this man is the one thing I knew I couldn't wait to do.

CHAPTER TWENTY-NINE

Forbidden Fruit

Now the serpent was more cunning than any beast of the field which the LORD God had made. And he said to the woman, "Has God indeed said, 'You shall not eat of every good tree of the garden?' And the woman said to the serpent, "We may eat the fruit of the trees of the garden, but of the fruit of the tree which is in the midst of the garden, God has said, 'You shall not eat it, nor shall you touch it, lest you die.'" Then the serpent said to the woman, "You will not surely die. For God knows that in the day you eat of it your eyes will be opened and you will be like God, knowing good and evil." So when the woman saw that the tree was good for food, that it was pleasant to the eyes, and a tree desirable to make one wise, she took of its fruit and ate. She also gave to her husband with her, and he ate.

Genesis 3:1-6

THE FIRST YEAR of our marriage held the typical excitements and adjustments that most newly married people experience; the only difference was that for us, it included functioning as an immediate family. We began and remained in Randy's little house on the west side of Indianapolis for the first few years of our marriage, securing the foundation of our relationship and welcoming the newest addition to our family.

A year after marrying Randy God blessed us with a daughter, and once again, as if on replay, I entered the delivery room believing her name would be Rebekah Elizabeth. It took one look at her to know that while the name Rebekah represented a beautiful servant for the Lord, that name didn't apply to this little princess. She wasn't a "Rebekah" ...we couldn't see calling her that two, three or ten years down the road.

I remember the two of us watching her, somehow feisty from her first breath, as if she was trying to subtly announce she had arrived and had come with a mission. "She's not a Rebekah," Randy said, looking at me.

Reflecting on what I had experienced with Matthew, I said, "No...she's not."

I was just beginning to understand the power that lies in a name, and my prayers had started to include asking God for Matthew to inherit the meaning of his name. I knew that whatever we named her would have to reflect the essence of who God had created her to be so that she too would one day embody its meaning. I watched her wriggle, arms flailing with little control, as if she were trying to get comfortable in her new surroundings and compared this moment to my previous experience. Already her personality was so different than

Matt's—she was far more vocal.

"What about Anna (Aunah), from Luke?" asked Randy.

"Hmmm, possibly. Why her?" I asked.

"She was a prophetess, widowed very young so she consecrated herself to the Lord, living her life at the Temple and served the Lord through praying and fasting. She was the one who bore witness of who Jesus was to the people of Israel when he was just days old."

I sat still for a moment longer watching her. Something about that name registered in our spirits and we knew that was it. And while we had no idea what her days would hold, the meaning of her name seemed to encapsulate this little one's essence. There was a subtle strength about her—a dignity in her little being that deserved to be acknowledged with a name that stood out from all the others, just like her namesake had separated herself from her generation. "I like it. Anna…Anna Marie Williams."

Adding Anna to our family made life feel fairly complete; we were happily married with two children, one of each sex, and I was able to stay at home full time. The only thing we didn't have was a white picket fence to complement our little two-bedroom 1940 bungalow. Located in a small, independent community near Indianapolis, the town was broken down into four distinct neighborhoods with each particular area having its own elementary school within walking distance of the residents. There were no busses or working cafeterias within the schools, which allowed the students to come home for lunch. Living there was like being transported back to a simpler time when most everyone around shared the values and ideas about life that we held so dear.

For the first time since high school, before my mother and I had moved to Indiana, I began to feel my roots relax and sink into the ground. I enjoyed watching Matthew establish friendships with other neighborhood boys, and I began to develop a few of my own. The only challenge we faced was the reality that our home was becoming noticeably smaller as our family continued to expand in number. Because of the high market demand of the area in which we lived, finding something bigger within our community would most likely be out of our price range.

Faced with seemingly few options, we began to pray and ask for God's help with the situation, not really understanding what He meant when He said, *"Indeed He would have brought you out of dire distress, into a broad place where there is no restraint; and what is set on your table would be full of richness"* (Job 36:16). We had believed it was *our* responsibility to find a house in an area where *we* wanted to live and then *we* would ask God to bless *our* decision and help with the process— never did we understand or realize that our focus was entirely on our own ability while the scripture focuses all on His.

It was late spring after we had celebrated Anna's second birthday and Matthew was almost finished with the first grade when we began to seriously explore our options. Preferring to stay within our community, we continually searched and looked at every available home in each of the four distinct districts, only to ultimately eliminate them from our search due to something just not "feeling right" about each one.

This process continued for months until it was nearly mid-summer and the pressure of time was closing in on us. The thought of transferring Matthew after school started seemed to add additional stress to our confined living space until our "need" became our driving force. After three months of nonproductive searches within our own small town, we decided to enlarge our boundary lines to include a much larger area just outside our community where Randy had grown up.

We spent the next few weeks driving through the various housing additions trying to identify what we liked and didn't like about each one. Yet it wasn't until we drove through a particular neighborhood in late July that we saw a For Sale sign in the front yard of a brick ranch home located in the middle of a cul-de-sac that caught our attention. I looked out the car window and something about that house reminded me of a home in Ohio where I had spent a fair amount of time as a teenager. It felt as if I was looking at that house, in that neighborhood, and the stability I had always longed for in Ohio suddenly seemed within my reach.

I looked at the neighboring houses and the quiet parklike setting of the cul-de-sac, trying to visualize our kids playing in the yard, when instantly a flash of memory reminded me how I used to feel whenever I spent time at my friend's house in Ohio. Every time I was there I had a sense of stability, as if it wasn't going anywhere, and I silently acknowledged how much I needed for my children to have that same experience.

I turned my head to look at Randy and, wanting his perspective, asked, "What do you think?"

"Well...I like the outside of it. And I love the lot."

I smiled, a bit reluctant to show too much emotion. "I really like this house, Randy. Can we look at it?"

At the nod of his head in agreement, I scrambled through my purse for a pen to write down the phone number. As he began to pull away from the house, Randy shared details about the school system, explaining it was one of the largest in the state. Thoughts of my earlier days in high school when I first transferred to Indiana and the shock caused by the enormity of the school and the kind of conversations that occurred among my new friends consumed my mind. I began the familiar mental journey with Silence as I analyzed whether or not I was too naïve when I moved as a teenager; perhaps if I had grown up in the city or with more people around I would have handled things better.

Interrupting my silent escapade, Randy pointed out the elementary school Matthew would attend if we bought that house. "He'll have to take a bus, Kel. How do you feel about that?"

The only reference point I had was the two months I had ridden the bus during my first stint in Indiana. "I don't know, Randy. I hated the bus."

"Yeah, but the school is so close to the house his ride would only be five or ten minutes."

I acknowledged his comment in silence then began to quietly argue with my doubts that were associated with large schools and busses, failing to recognize them as "checks in my spirit," or unrest in my soul. I just thought perhaps they were merely obstacles that needed to be overcome if I really wanted the reassurance that would come from living in that home. By the time we actually looked at the house and decided to make an offer on it, our living there became less about gaining the necessary space and more about what the house actually represented to me.

My thoughts became increasingly occupied with visions

of family life in that house and Christmas mornings spent in front of the fireplace. Within a matter of days I had crafted an incredible Normal Rockwell image of what the great American family would look like living on that quiet cul-de-sac. The thought was captivating and enticing all at once so when Randy came to me stating he believed the Lord had given him a price point he was not to exceed, I was skeptical at best. Subtly convinced that my imaginary utopia had come straight from God, I quickly disregarded Randy's financial limitation until I dismissed him altogether.

The negotiations dragged on over the next week as the owner countered and we made our counteroffers. Convinced that the Lord wanted to bless us with this home, I asked friends to agree with us in prayer for this house, and didn't know exactly how to react when one of them finally said, "Kelly, with all the back and forth going on, are you sure this is the house the Lord has for you?"

I felt my forehead crease in confusion at the absurdity of her question and stammered out, "Well…uh, yes. Why would you think that?"

"Well, Jesus said His burden is easy and His yoke is light. To be honest, none of this feels easy or light, which makes me wonder if the Lord's really in it."

As if her spoken words had hit me and bounced back off, I responded with a fairly quick and defensive retort, "No, I just think it's the enemy trying to thwart what God wants. He's just putting barricades in the way. God's heart is for us to have this house …why wouldn't He?" spoken more rhetorically than actually wanting an answer.

Shrugging her shoulders she appeared to concede to my

logic, then smirked and said, "Okay," walking away.

As I considered my statements, what I had uttered as a rhetorical question began to sound more like a challenge, "Of course God wants me to have this house. It's everything I've ever wanted."

I fought to dismiss her verbal dispute and put it in the same category where those other nagging thoughts about school size and busses resided. I reassured myself with silent utterances, *It'll be worth it when we move in and get settled. They'll see.*

When I came home later that evening Randy informed me that an agreement couldn't be reached between him and the owners, explaining they wanted more than he was willing to pay.

"How much more?" I asked

"Does it matter? I really believe the Lord gave me that amount, Kel. I'm not going over it."

I was shocked, "Are you kidding? You're going to lose that house over, what, a couple thousand dollars?"

Randy took a deep inhale, "Kelly, it's not the amount. It's the principle."

"I don't understand. Can we not afford the difference in the payment?"

The argument continued for days, but no matter how much support I had for wanting the house, Randy wouldn't buckle. To make matters worse, just about the time I considered relenting in my pursuit, school registration was looming and I felt like I was in a pressure cooker. We needed more room, we loved the house, and frankly, his logic made no sense to me. I continued to battle him until one day he showed just the slightest bit of weakness and, like a shark smells blood, I could sense his vulnerability. I kept presenting my case until I, like Eve, convinced him to partake in the apple and he, like Adam, chose to go against what the Lord had said.

Randy met the owners' counteroffer by agreeing to pay the additional amount over what the Lord had spoken to him, and he did it just in time to register Matthew at the new school. I was elated and in my mind the Lord was victorious, regardless of the pesky doubts that remained lurking in the deepest recesses of my spirit. The only other issue that needed resolved was the earnest money necessary to secure the offer.

We had saved half of what the owners were requiring, and what clearly should have been seen as another warning sign from the Lord was somehow interpreted as hindrance from the enemy. Convinced that we needed to push through, I asked Randy what the harm was in borrowing the remaining balance from a friend since we knew we could pay it back after closing. "It's just temporary, Randy. It's no big deal," I argued.

Although I was successful in convincing Randy to borrow the money from a family friend the next day and we signed the Purchase Agreement later that afternoon, something about it was bittersweet. Like a blessing that you had to beg for, there was little victory to be shared on the way home from the signing. Instead, after we returned home, when we should have been ecstatic about our "victory," I sat on the front steps of the porch and watched Randy pound the "For Sale by Owner" sign in our front yard and told myself, *This is it.*

I pictured us living in the new house and tried to find comfort with the Normal Rockwell way of life I had dreamt about, but something about the simplicity of our little home seemed to beckon me. I looked down the street and thought about making friends with the other mothers, and as the leaves of the trees overhead waved in the summer breeze, I savored the feeling of finally blending in and being a part of something again. I was at peace here.

The sound of the hammer striking the stake called me out of my reflection. *You're so dramatic*, I told myself. Standing up I brushed myself clean as if I was trying to wipe off my hesitations, and watched as Randy straightened out the sign. *Everyone feels this way when they leave their first home. Of course, you're sad—this is where it all began for you and Randy*, my inner conversation continued. *You'll be fine*, I reassured myself. *Really.*

CHAPTER THIRTY

Bittersweet Realities

Like a bird wanders from its nest is a man
who wanders from his place.
Proverbs 27:8

WEEKS PASSED AND little interest was shown in our home. We didn't understand because the community where Randy and I lived was considered to be a proverbial hotspot in the city. Quaint neighborhoods, excellent schools, and low taxes all contributed toward a thriving housing market and homes were sold often merely by word of mouth. It was very rare to even see a For Sale sign in a yard. The inability to sell our home, especially with a For Sale sign, was an unexpected difficulty that required us to reexamine our options.

I've often wondered if my friend's earlier counsel about Jesus' burden being easy and His yoke light had penetrated my spirit when she said it, if I would have perceived this latest challenge as another spiritual warning sign, but admittedly I didn't. I didn't have the spiritual sense to recognize that when God shuts a door, one shouldn't force it back open. Isaiah once said, "So he shall open, and no one shall shut; and he shall shut, and no one shall open" (22:22).

Unbeknownst to me, something had prevented my "eyes" from seeing these particular barricades as closed doors, despite what wise counsel was trying to tell me. Rather, I chose to view them as opportunities to fight harder, as if the Lord's desire was to strengthen my resolve to fight for what I believed He wanted us to have.

As time droned on, the idea of living in that house grew in scope and measure. I could think of nothing else except the grandeur that came from creating the ideal family residence. I was steadfast in my commitment to create a world for my children that I had always wanted, especially the stability and stature that would come from living in that type of a house. I never associated the weight of that vision as pressure; it was incentive. Just like the impending start of school and the risk of losing our earnest money if our house didn't sell, these were merely reasons for us to get more aggressive. So after three weeks of trying to sell our home without a realtor, I began to once again challenge our original plan.

Even though I was fully aware of our promise to each other that if our house didn't sell we would interpret that as God saying no, when it actually became a reality I couldn't concede to what I viewed as failure. I couldn't entertain let alone accept the thought of not living in that house; after all we had fought for, there was no way God wouldn't want us to have it. So, just like before, I began to plead, persuade and pressure until

I ultimately convinced Randy to list the house with a realtor. Days later, the "door" flew open with an offer that we accepted, and our home was sold. The moment Randy hung up the phone and announced the news, a sense of surreality, almost sadness, engulfed the room and I silently questioned why I wasn't more excited. *I thought victories called for celebrations... I don't feel very victorious*, I told myself.

Not knowing what to do with my internal conflict, I halfheartedly smiled at Randy and went into Matthew and Anna's room. Walking through our little house was different as soon as I knew it wasn't really ours anymore. I thought about that first night with Randy, four years ago, when he brought me here to listen to his favorite song, then how the three of us decorated our first Christmas tree the year we were married. Sitting on Matt's bed, I looked out their window and remembered pulling into the driveway when we brought Anna home from the hospital—the three years felt like they had flown by. I sat a little deeper as I watched my children play nearby and thought, *I feel safe here...stable...secure.*

Then a second, smaller thought seemed to race through my mind, whispering, *It isn't too late. You can always change your mind.*

Sitting up as if drawn to attention, I shook my head in confusion then dismissed the thought. *It's too late for that*, I told myself. I couldn't voice my doubts. I had fought entirely too hard.

CHAPTER THIRTY-ONE

Unexpected Changes

THE CLOSING DATE was set and our house was gradually becoming less and less ours as things were being slowly sorted and packed. I struggled to have the energy to get things done and often got taken over by a flu that didn't seem to want to leave me alone. I fought to keep up with everything, but figured that once I got settled in the new place I would be fine, so I pressed on.

A foreboding sense filled the car as Randy and I drove to closing. Something didn't feel quite right, but neither of us could clearly identify it. I knew we should be excited about moving in, but the thought of turning over the keys to our old house seemed to overshadow every other emotion. I wanted to resent the new owners and found myself jealous of them at signing, only to wonder what was wrong with me. I knew I should have been happy, but I wasn't. I wasn't happy and I didn't feel well.

When the mortgage officer announced that we had finally come to the end of the stack and were ready to sign the last piece of paper, the room fell strangely silent. I felt my fingers grip the chair as I tried to disguise my conflicting emotions. I knew better than to say anything and tried to smile, hoping to mask my regret. We had agreed to surrender the keys the following Saturday, one week before the start of school. I sank in the chair. I didn't want to move—I wanted to scream, "No, I take it back! I want my little house in my little neighborhood. I want Matthew in his little school—I don't want him on a bus!"

But instead I just sat there, Silence summoning me. I was going to be sick. I tried to politely excuse myself and left to find a bathroom as Randy finalized the details.

"What is wrong, Kelly?" Randy asked as he pulled back into our driveway.

"I just don't feel well," I replied.

Reluctant to accept my answer he pressed, "Are you sure that's all?"

He looked at me as if his eyes could find the truth. I wanted to say, "I hate when you do that," but shoved that thought back down and instead nodded my head and said, "Yeah, I'm sure," and silently went in the house.

I protected myself from my inner ambush by playing with the kids until it was time to volunteer at the Crisis Pregnancy Center later that day. Being there was always medicinal for me, so I looked forward to seeing the other counselors and being with clients. However, it was a slow night, and little distraction was found from my regret or my nausea. I sat at the desk twirling a pencil back and forth and stared at the calendar.

Life really is good, Kel... I tried to tell myself.

I thought about the vacation we took to Myrtle Beach at the end of June, and then counted how many days had passed since we attended a cousin's wedding in Ohio. *When was my last period?* I wondered. I sat up and pulled the desk calendar closer and began counting backwards. I remember preparing and packing in case I started but realized I never did, so I kept counting, all the way back to the end of May. "Uh oh, it's already August."

An all too familiar pit began to form in my stomach. *How can this happen,* I asked myself. I knew how it happened, but couldn't figure out how I could be pregnant when I was on the Pill. Shaking my head in confusion, I stood up figuring I was in the best place to find the answer I needed. I walked to the bathroom, grabbing a pregnancy test along the way.

It took minutes for me to see the little plus sign appear in the window. I stood there stunned, muttering inaudibly, "You have got to be kidding me," not sure who I was talking to other than myself. Although it explained my unending "flu," I wasn't prepared for this. The stress of the day was mounting and began to win my battle for composure.

I sat back down on the toilet lid, bent over and just cried; I didn't know what else to do. Nothing was going as I had planned. The reality that I was moving out of a community I loved to live in a house I didn't want and was all of a sudden potentially too small without ever having lived there washed over me...and all on closing day. I shook my head in sheer disbelief, wondering when and where things had gotten so off kilter. All my desperation and frustration came pouring out and I knew I wouldn't be of any value to anyone that evening;

I needed to go home.

The time it took for me to pull out of the parking lot was all I needed before the accumulative emotions of the day surfaced again. Remorse, regret, confusion, and fear pummeled my soul as I questioned for the second time in my life, *How did I get here?*

In desperation, I repeatedly asked myself, *What am I going to do?* knowing full well there were no real options. Fear began to seep into the car as I mentally rehearsed telling Randy, wondering how he would react. I tried not to think about the last time I had to share the news of an unplanned pregnancy, then questioned if I would always feel defined by that experience. *Will it always be a marker in my life, Lord?*

By the time I turned the corner, my imaginary conversation had propelled me into a breathless state. In a feeble effort to collect myself, I sat in the car watching Randy throw a ball to Matt and Anna in the front yard until he motioned to the kids to play together. I gathered my things, worked my way out of the car and walked up the driveway. "You're home early. Is everything okay?" he asked.

Fighting to take in air, my rehearsed presentation erased itself from my memory and I blurted out, "I was at the Center... and we weren't busy... so I started thinking."

Confused, he continued to look at me, "And?"

"Well, I realized it's been awhile since I started ... so I took a pregnancy test." I collected my thoughts long enough to pause to see if I could detect a reaction from him. I'm not sure what I expected, but I braced myself for disappointment or disapproval to appear. Instead his facial expression never wavered from anything but concern for me. I felt his fingers search for mine. "And? What did it say?" he continued.

The tenderness in his voice made it easier to breathe. I found myself willing to step out from the shadow of Fear a bit further. I exhaled. "It was positive ... I'm pregnant."

For a split second Randy closed his eyes, then slowly grinned. I felt him squeeze my hand and, for just a moment, silence hung between us. I wasn't sure what he was thinking but he seemed fine. I stood still, waiting to hear what he was going to say, when finally he opened his eyes, looked at me, grinned then said, "Well...this could be fun."

CHAPTER THIRTY-TWO

Even Forgiven Sins Have Consequences

THE DAY WE moved into the house felt as if invisible shackles were being slapped on my spirit. Although I knew I should have been excited about "winning a long hard-fought battle," the victory was somehow being consumed by a sense of dread and regret, although I didn't fully understand why. I had been so convinced that God wanted us to have this house; why did I keep imagining ways to keep the keys to our old one? I felt like a captive being dragged away, screaming for someone to jump in and say it was all a mistake. The only problem was I had no voice with which to cry out—Silence had returned.

I stood in the front room looking out the bay window, watching people unload our belongings. *How ironic*, I told myself. *You used to feel like Tamar—now you know what*

Amnon felt like after he had taken Tamar against her will. His hate grew to be far greater for her than the love he thought he had originally felt. ... I stopped and asked myself, *Could it be that the so called love that had propelled me to manipulate everyone around me so I could buy this house was slowly evolving into a burning hatred for the very object I had once coveted?* I allowed the sudden realization to sink in, but my newfound awareness sickened me.

Looking around the empty room, I yearned to return to my little house in my little community. I tried to devise a plan that would allow me to return things to where they rightfully belonged and immediately recognized this growing feeling of remorse. Visions of leaving Ohio for the last time began flashing in my head, and I saw pieces of my heart lying scattered along the road just like the bread crumb trail Hansel and Gretel had left in the woods in an innocent attempt to help them find their way back home. I sat down on the hearth and fought the tightening of my throat.

I felt like Eve hiding in the bushes after she had taken a bite of the apple and waited to hear the Lord ask me, "What is this that you have done?" (Genesis 3:13), but nothing came. I shuddered at the thought of all I had given up and wondered how I was going to tell Randy I was wrong; I didn't want this house. He had done everything I asked him, and now all I wanted is what we had, but there was no getting back my "birthright" (Genesis 25:31- 32)—I had just sold it.

I closed my eyes and reviewed my options. *Now what?* I quietly asked myself. Sensing I would wear the shackles of regret for the unforeseeable future, I tried convincing myself that the only available option for the time being was to come to terms with what I had done and make the best of it, for I had been hemmed in by my own volition and left with no other choice.

The testing of that decision occurred within the first week of our living there as I stood at the end of the driveway, Anna in my arms, trying to dissect the foreign feeling in my stomach that surfaced as Matthew boarded the school bus. I was used to a neighborhood where the children walked safely back and forth to school; in comparison, this act felt so impersonal. We waited for the doors to close, and as I picked Anna up to wave goodbye I thought about his other friends starting their school day and waving goodbye to their parents and wondered if they missed him. Watching for his little face to peer out of the window so we could say our silent goodbyes, I ached for him to be a part of that other world.

The day passed painfully slowly waiting for Matthew to return home and share his account of his school day. As soon as we heard the bus' brakes squeal, Anna and I raced to meet him at the bottom of the drive. I watched as my usually lighthearted, happy young son slumbered down the bus steps with his shoulders slouched and his backpack dragging behind him as if he didn't have enough energy to even look up. Waiting until his feet hit the ground, I tousled his hair and asked, "How'd it go, buddy?"

With a shrug of his shoulders Matthew continued up the driveway, dragging his feet with every step. The day had visibly affected him. I wanted to assume it was because of the change in schools and friends, but when he shared his account of being spat upon earlier that day and how the students wouldn't listen to the teacher's instructions—instead they called her names and told her to shut up—I felt like the shade on a window had been snapped open without warning. I was stunned by the starkness of the different environment and wasn't prepared to answer his questions about why somebody would behave like that or why some students were permitted to be disrespectful.

My heart began to grieve anew for the innocence of what we had left behind, and as Matthew grew increasingly silent, Jesus' words from John 10:10 came to me, stopping me in my tracks: *"The thief does not come except to steal, and to kill, and to destroy…"* Not moving, I looked up at the house—the house that just two months ago seemed to beckon me relentlessly, wrapped up with an imaginary bow that on the surface had all the appearances it was from God Himself, and I wondered just what exactly the enemy wanted to steal, kill and destroy in us.

Standing in the middle of the driveway I watched my son's deflated spirit enter the house and couldn't help but think about Eve. Initially she was so excited, so confident to share her new discovery with Adam and convince him to partake with her, and yet I couldn't help but wonder, had she known how differently she would feel afterward, would she have opted to undo her actions if given the opportunity? Undoubtedly she must have been overwhelmed by her emotions because they sent her into hiding (Genesis 3:10), consumed with her shame and fear of a God who had never once given her reason to be afraid. *Funny how sin penetrates and distorts our perceptions,* I thought.

Minutes later my brain started to will my feet to move. As I approached the front door, I thought it oddly peculiar how the only way we have come to experience God's infinite grace and mercy is through Adam and Eve's deception and subsequent act of disobedience. Closing the door behind me, I never considered how He might use my own act of spiritual rebellion to intimately introduce me to His character in such a way that would forever alter how I lived my life, both spiritually and in the natural.

CHAPTER THIRTY-THREE

Internal Transformation

Honor your father and your mother,
that your days may be long upon the land which
the LORD your God is giving you.
Exodus 20:12

SEVEN MONTHS HAD passed since we had moved, and the baby's birth was imminent. Over the initial shock of the surprise, Randy and I were counting the days until his arrival, realizing our hands—and our house—would be more than full. In the interim, we focused on learning how to effectively deal with the ongoing challenges Matthew was encountering at school, as well as the emerging strain our financial state was beginning to create as a result of our impending arrival.

Within weeks of learning we were pregnant and moving to the new house we discovered that due to Randy's self employment status, maternity coverage was not part of our insurance plan; therefore our unexpected bundle of joy would be termed a "Cash Baby." And although the doctors and hospitals were generous with their discounts, the reality was that any money we had saved toward Randy's self-employment taxes would now have to be used to pay for the birth of the baby, causing us in turn to second mortgage the house to pay the taxes. In short, come April our monthly financial outlay would greatly exceed our budgeted monthly intake and we weren't exactly sure how things were going to work out.

Gone were the days of familiar routine and predictable outcomes. Instead it felt like we were living life in unexplored territory that held unexpected obstacles so huge we couldn't see our way around them. All we really knew to do was hold on to each other and center our attention on our family. We prepared, packed and counted the days until the baby's arrival, and having entered the delivery room twice before, I knew to have more than one potential name selected. So armed and ready I went fully expecting things to play out as they did when Anna was born. Unbeknownst to me this time, however, Randy asked my mother to join us in the delivery room. Reflecting back, I believe having both he and my mother there was the final detail—like the bow on a package—of how very far God had brought me.

It was 7:35 a.m. on February 22 when Aaron entered this world and took his first breath. Despite his unplanned arrival, I marveled at how beautifully woven together our family's story was becoming. Watching him squirm under the bright lights of his little hospital bed I was struck by the thought that planned or not, his very presence had already made our family feel complete on some level. Randy and I watched as they tested and weighed him and, without a word, instinctively knew that his 10 pound, 2 ounce frame was sent here so that he would make a statement amid his generation—therefore he needed to make a statement with his name.

Holding him, we marveled at his size as evidenced by the fullness of his face and the roundness of his body and knew immediately that between the names we had pondered, he wasn't a "Jordan"—that name would have been misplaced on him. And though we can't fully explain it, our sense told us he had been given an inner strength that would take years to fashion and mold. He deserved the name that would personify that strength; his name would be Aaron—a mountain of strength, a mediator for his people. Added to that strength would be his father's middle name, Michael, for we believed him to be a warrior for the Lord. His name would be Aaron Michael, and with that I asked the Lord to give him his father's kindness, his dignity and his incredibly gentle spirit. And selfishly, I prayed he would bear his good looks.

Bringing Aaron home and settling into a new routine with a now three year old and an eight year old took some adjustment, but not much time. By late spring our new way of life had taken over, bringing with it Matthew's emerging quest for identity as evidenced by his innumerable questions. Having to revisit my unresolved past would inevitably lead me toward the land of regret, and I often would stop to dwell on the early days before first moving to Indiana, the days before everything spiraled out of control when I was whole and intact living with my mother.

If I allowed my mind to freely roam, I could identify two distinct markers that forever altered the course of my life: The first was the day my mother told me she was staying in Indiana. The second was my engaging in an unhealthy relationship—one that seemed to have a finger system that crept into every area of my life, burrowing trenches all along the way. While I could identify these markers, I didn't have any idea how to loosen the grip they held over my spirit. I believed them to be things that just "were," like indistinguishable moments in time that I believed I couldn't really do anything about. I completely bought into the lie that "you just live with it."

Although I was immersed in church life, as Beth Moore says, my theology had not yet truly penetrated my reality. There was no power behind what I believed because though I would read the Scriptures, something was prohibiting God's breath to flow over them. For example, Mark 5:24-34 says,

> So Jesus went with him, and a great multitude followed Him and thronged Him. Now a certain woman had a flow of blood for twelve years, and had suffered many things from many physicians. She had spent all that she had and was no better, but rather grew worse. When she heard about Jesus, she came behind Him in the crowd and touched His garment. For she said, "If only I may touch His clothes, I shall be made well." Immediately the fountain of her blood was dried up, and she felt in her body that she was healed of the affliction. And Jesus, immediately knowing in Himself that power had gone out of Him, turned around in the crowd and said, "Who touched my clothes?" But His disciples said to Him, "You see the multitude thronging You, and You say, 'Who touched Me?'" And He looked around to see her who had done this thing. But the woman, fearing and trembling, knowing what had happened to her,

came and fell down before Him and told Him the whole truth. And He said to her, "Daughter, your faith has made you well. Go in peace, and be healed of your affliction."

When I first read this account, the story seemed to be a powerful demonstration of Jesus' kindness and ability to heal, and perhaps those who have suffered with chronic pain or illness can more deeply identify with the physical, emotional and financial drain the woman's illness may have taken on her being.

Yet for those of us whose disease lies under the surface and remains visibly undetectable, it often takes more time to realize how exhausting it is to carry the weight of our own affliction. It has been my experience that most of us don't find ourselves desperate enough to press through the crowds until, like the woman in Mark, we have exhausted all other efforts to function "normally" and have no other place to go except to the One we have heard about.

In other words, since those first days in that house I have come to understand that in one way this passage is intended to encourage those of us who need healing from that which has perhaps plagued us for countless years or is new and fresh but is intended to destroy us just the same. Because healing—whether physical, emotional, mental or spiritual— is something we often only obtain by pressing into the very difficulties that threaten to consume us so that we can find Jesus in their midst.

Mark states in verse 24, "*So Jesus went with him, and a great multitude followed Him and thronged Him.*" The word "thronged" has been described as a "pushing, shoving, elbowing crowd"—what we might see at Times Square on New Year's Eve. The streets were jammed with people pressing and fighting to see Jesus, and this woman who had an issue with blood loss for twelve years resulting in an indescribable physical and emotional weakness, pressed her way through insurmountable odds toward the one Person she knew—she didn't just believe but *knew*—would heal her.

Unlike the woman in Mark, I could identify the source of my spiritual and emotional bleeding; I just didn't understand exactly how to *press* through the crowd. Truth being, I couldn't really even recognize the things that seemed to stand in my way. Instead I would find myself confronted with road blocks barricading my path, encouraging me to find someone else to blame so I could finagle my way around the obstruction.

Over time, I had successfully convinced myself that had my mother chosen to come back to Ohio like she said she would, my life would have been entirely different. Blaming her somehow justified my contribution to the situation, making it progressively easier to place the burden of what happened to me at her feet because the reoccurring accusation "she left you" was never very far from my thought life.

Subsequently it should have come as no surprise that God would use Matthew's quest for identity as the means to take me back to the root of my own seemingly justifiable heart condition toward my mother. Having been invited by another couple, our mentors, to attend a traditional basketball event in downtown Indianapolis, Randy and I had looked forward to the free evening for some time. So amid thousands of other people all abuzz with excitement, the four of us entered Market Square Arena and waited for the event to start.

The atmosphere was light between us, and finding things to talk about never really posed a challenge. So once we found our seats and Matthew's name came up, both Randy and I were fairly transparent about where things stood. "We were seeking counsel, and believed at this point we would meet with his biological father and ask for pictures rather than allow Matthew to meet him." It just wasn't time. The conversation stilled for a moment when I heard Scott ask me, "How are you doing with all this, Kelly?"

Taken back by the unexpected arrow that I just felt hit my heart, I quickly said, "Fine" in a dismissive tone that communicated far more than the single uttered word. Scott continued, "Are you sure? You don't seem fine."

Silence joined us. I looked to Randy for guidance, but before he could answer Scott pressed, "What is it, Kelly?"

I looked down and watched my fingers spin my ring. When I looked up all I could mutter was, "I don't know" with a shrug of my shoulders.

The crowds began to fill the seats around us and the conversation gradually minimized to the point that only Scott and I could accurately hear each other. "It's just sometimes I resent having to go back. It always ends up with me imagining how things would have turned out if my mother had come home like she said she would. I don't know…maybe I wouldn't have gotten pregnant."

No sooner was it out than regret washed over me. "It's not that I don't want Matt—I do. I just feel robbed, like I've missed out on things. My whole life changed."

"Did your mom ever meet him, Matthew's biological father?" Scott asked.

Vivid memories of that day immediately swarmed my mind. "Oh yeah, she met him. She DID NOT like him."

"Why? What did she say?"

Reflecting back I said, "I don't know why. She said he was trouble … warned me to stay away from him."

"How long before she knew you didn't listen?" he asked.

"Hmmm…she knew from the beginning because I asked her if I could have dinner with him and she said no. I argued with her and when she wouldn't buckle, I finally told her, 'You didn't care enough about me to come home, don't care enough about me to tell me what to do now,' then I hung up on her."

Scott was quiet for a few moments and I sat there, on some level feeling satisfied as if I had accurately ascribed responsibility right where it belonged. I looked at him when I heard him clear his throat and immediately sensed his struggle to search for words. "Kelly, when Jesus sent the disciples out in Luke 10, how did He send them?"

"That's an odd question—He sent them in twos. Why?"

"How many times did your mother warn you about him?" Scott asked.

Suspicious of where he was going with this, I felt my heart sink—quietly I said, "Two."

"Kelly…you didn't get pregnant because your mother didn't come home or because she left you. You got pregnant because you rebelled and didn't listen to her. She warned you twice, right?" he asked.

I nodded my head in silent agreement. He continued, "We are called to honor our fathers and mothers. Kelly…you didn't honor your mother."

The truth behind his words forced me to lean back in my

seat, silent, and I knew that in the midst of the crowd the Lord had just passed by. Unable to completely grasp the enormity of it, all I could utter was, "Oh my God." Conviction for my heart's attitude toward my mother began to consume me, "Oh Lord, I'm sorry," I mumbled, holding my head in my hands.

Those first days of loneliness replayed in my mind—living as an only child with my stepfather, yearning for fellowship and laughter. The magnitude of it all washed over me. Then like a systematic chain of events, for the first time I began to realize the choices that were mine to make. I could have chosen differently: I could have returned to Indiana and lived with my mother, and I most certainly could have chosen to not get involved in a relationship I knew I should have avoided.

Suddenly I allowed the flashing warning signs to reappear as I remembered how I felt when he first called to ask me out and I said no, then again having to work to disregard the voice that kept saying, "You shouldn't do this" when I learned he was married.

Like a long lost friend I hadn't seen in awhile, I recognized those "checks in my spirit" as warnings from the Lord and wanted to groan in despair for having not heeded their caution. I tried to counter the pain by offering my "mitigating circumstances" as a defense, but the conviction wouldn't leave me alone. Scott was right, and if there was any hope of overcoming the grip of unforgiveness I held toward my mother, I was going to have to stand in this place and repent. I closed my eyes and allowed myself to become a silent one of thousands amid the surrounding crowd emulating the noise of the gathering I had read about in Mark … I imagined myself pressing against them, stretching out, straining to hold on to this newfound truth, believing that by doing so, I would actually be touching the hem of His garment and thereby find healing.

CHAPTER THIRTY-FOUR

Theology Hits Reality

And have no fellowship with the unfruitful
works of darkness, but rather expose them. For
it is shameful even to speak of those things
which are done by them in secret. But all
things that are exposed are made manifest by
the light, for whatever makes manifest is light.
Ephesians 5:11-13

THERE ARE TIMES when the Lord chooses, as He did for the
woman who had the bleeding disorder, to immediately heal the
one who seeks Him, while other times He requires us to join
in the miracle and heals us through a process such as Naaman
in 2 Kings 5:14: "So he went down and dipped seven times in
the Jordan, according to the saying of the man of God; and his
flesh was restored like the flesh of a little child, and he was
clean." Or again in John 9 when Jesus made clay with His
saliva and anointed the eyes of the blind man with the clay and

said to him, "Go, wash in the pool of Soloam." We have come to define these moments as "poof or process" in our home, and more often than not the Lord has chosen to heal me gradually through process, always remaining faithful to reveal Himself all along the way.

So it was through my conversation with Scott. Although truth went forth that evening, undoubtedly the Lord required me to walk the process out in obedience before it would have its full and whole effect on my spirit. Hearing and standing in the truth regarding my time in Ohio caused three things to ultimately occur:

1) It required **me** to acknowledge and take responsibility for **my** decisions and actions;

2) He brought me to a place where I could acknowledge and repent for dishonoring my mother, and

3) I experienced forgiveness for blaming my mother, thereby releasing the Spirit of unforgiveness that had bound me.

None of these things came quickly or easily, and there were often times I had to remind myself that this is what "pressing through the crowd" feels like. Resistance came from all angles and certainly the easier route would have been to hold onto my "abandonment" and use it as a justifier for my choices—after all, to stand before the LORD, like Adam and Eve once did, naked and not ashamed (Gen. 2:25) isn't possible unless we have a covering. Initially, I wanted mine to be in the form of blaming my mother, as if pointing out the fallacy of her decision was a sufficient excuse for my own choices. When in reality, it wasn't until the Lord confronted my soul with the truth of what *I* had done, with no defense or excuse, that I could truly accept the covering He was offering me through the cross of Christ—that was the moment when my theology first hit my reality, right in the center of my story.

All of this took an immeasurable amount of time, and as I made feeble attempts to not stumble along the way, by the time we were preparing to celebrate Matthew's ninth birthday I was about to discover the road I had been walking was the precursor to where the Lord was really leading me.

In light of Matthew's natural curiosity, Randy and I began dealing with the reality that Matthew may very well insist on meeting his biological father, which was a paralyzing thought for me. Having been deliberate in telling Matthew the truth from his earliest days before Randy, actually discussing the situation held no viable fear for me. Our minute conversations began when he was just a toddler and would ask, "Mommy, I don't have a daddy, do I?" And I would quickly respond, "Oh, you do, honey. It's just that he's in Ohio with his other family."

Oblivious to life any differently, that answer always seemed to satisfy him. Then when Randy and I decided to get married, Matthew, barely four at the time, made the decision that he would wait to call Randy "Daddy" until after we were married. To this day, he can't explain why; it's just the way it was for him. Now too, there were things that he couldn't fully explain, including his struggle to understand himself. Although different for boys than perhaps girls, my own life experience gave me some intimate knowledge of how it felt to wonder what life would have been like if my father were around. Perhaps inquiries such as "Why do I react this way?" or "Who do I really look like?" wouldn't have been quite so unending if he had been physically present. Hence, as a result of my own internal struggle, my heart became deeply committed to cause Matthew the least amount of pain as he searched for his own answers.

Therefore as Matthew's curiosity increased about who he looked like or what aspects of his personality belonged to whom, Randy and I were becoming more and more aware of the looming possibility that we would have to make contact with his biological father. With each pressing inquiry, it soon became a priority to guide Matthew through the potential landmine of uncertainties and help him avoid any major pitfalls by following a twofold approach:

1) Suggest to Matthew he write a letter and mail it. If he gets a response, then he can write another letter. If he doesn't receive anything in return, then only the portion of his heart that was given in the letter would be hurt; since it was less intrusive than an actual phone call, it seemed to be far less threatening to Matthew's development. And/or,

2) If Matthew requested pictures, they needed to be current since boys tend to make idols out of men closer to their age, and adoptive fathers like those in Randy's position don't need any additional or unwarranted competition that may come from an out of date picture.

Randy and I deliberated for quite some time over the options until we finally decided that if Matthew really wanted to make contact, we would help him write the letter and then cautiously prepare him for an unknown outcome. Surprisingly, when given the option Matthew declined, explaining he just wasn't that interested. "I really just want to know if I look like him."

Relieved yet stunned on some level, I was thankful to leave Matthew in his well protected cocoon yet fully aware that the thought of making contact left me completely paralyzed. Despite how simple it sounds on paper, taking the actual steps was a far more daunting task than I originally thought. Gone were all the preconceived ideas of what I would say to him if I was given the chance; instead, no matter how often Randy and I tried to devise a plan of action, Silence would immediately join our conversation, leaving me speechless and incapable of explaining my fears.

At first glance it appeared relatively easy—since I knew him it made sense for me to just call and ask. But something in Randy rose up and he became unusually insistent on being the one to make contact, citing he needed to "establish order because we're not just opening the door to Matt, we're potentially opening the door to our entire family." He strongly believed that although he knew *of* him, it would be best if he met him so he would have his own sense as to who and what he was actually dealing with in light of all that was at stake.

Having zero point of reference for a protective covering, I failed to understand the shield of defense that God was providing for both me and Matthew through Randy's involvement in the situation. Most often the torrent of a thousand thoughts would invade my mind every time Randy would approach the subject, and although I believed I had mastered the ability to camouflage my internal battle, the war waged deep within me. Moments of time would be spent idolizing the thought that my family was normal and my children all shared the same biological father. But then like a flashflood out of nowhere, I would hear the voice that dwelt with me in the cave saying,

"Yeah, but you'll get to see him—you know you want to." And then guilt would assault my mental betrayal of Randy.

Only I knew how far reaching the ache of regret in my soul went. While I no longer lived in a cave of darkness, the thought of my inner war not being exposed still held massive appeal. I tried to cover it with valiancy then dismissal, but somehow always managed to end up feeling like a tennis ball being hit back and forth—confident and assured of my feelings for Randy when I was on one side of the court, then consumed with all the plans and dreams I had once had of Ohio on the other side.

My own vain imagination had been cut loose once Randy set the time and date for the meeting, and for the first time in nearly ten years I felt like Pandora's Box had been opened and every emotion that I had locked away was fighting to get to the surface.

The playing out of my former dreams occurred only in my own mind, for shame would always prevent me from bringing things into the light. Even amid my truest confidants, I remained unable to give language to the deepest sources of my internal betrayal, resulting in the onslaught of newfound condemnation and abhorrence for my personal turmoil. I deeply wrestled with knowing and understanding how blessed I truly was with the character of Randy, but something in me remained connected to my former life and relationship in Ohio and wouldn't let go. So my only perceived option was to live openly in my gratitude and love for Randy, and fight to keep the remnants of Ohio hidden far below the surface.

Certainly I didn't understand at the time that one of the enemy's most effective weapons formed against us is shame—

in part, because shame draws its power by staying hidden. In my case, my own inability or unwillingness to verbalize my inner conflict empowered the enemy's grip of shame on my life. John 3:20-21 states, *"For everyone practicing evil hates the light and does not come to the light, lest his deeds should be exposed. But he who does the truth comes to the light, that his deeds may be clearly seen, that they have been done in God."*

Secondly, if the enemy can keep the true source of the battle undisclosed then the war will wage on and he remains in control of spiritual land he has no legal right to, in part because we remain unaware of who and what we are really fighting against. The apostle Paul states in 1 Corinthians 14:33, *"For God is not the author of confusion but of peace..."* Undoubtedly my spirit was encased in confusion and discord, yet I failed to recognize the driving force behind my battle. Instead I remained distracted and focused on the "wrong" behind the way I felt, and again, like Eve, the shame my thoughts produced drove me into hiding rather than calling me into the Light. I just didn't understand that conquering an enemy we keep hidden is nearly impossible.

As the days approached before our scheduled trip to Ohio, Randy and I were sitting at a red light near our home. Silence had once again joined me on my imaginary rehearsal of the upcoming meeting, and I found myself, though physically present, emotionally and mentally vacant from the car. I watched the raindrops race one another down the windshield and thought about the irony behind the weather—it was raining the day I left Ohio for the last time. "Some things never change, do they?" the raspy voice from the cave asked.

I felt Randy's hand squeeze mine as he said, "What are you thinking?"

Safely I responded, "Ohio."

The radio droned on as the light turned green. "You okay?" he asked.

I looked at him, offering a silent thank you that he couldn't hold my gaze for long. "Yeah, why?"

I could always tell when he was searching for words—not because he didn't know what to say but more out of intentionality with phrasing, and grace always his prime objective. "This is a big deal, Kel...it's understandable if you're afraid."

Trying to subtly avoid exposure, I asked, "Afraid?...Afraid of what?"

He slowed the car down as he turned the steering wheel toward the driveway, "I would think you're scared of how you feel. Are you afraid that you still love him?"

There it was. Exposed—out in the open—unveiled in one question, and all I could do was sit with Silence and try to figure out what to say. How do you tell your husband of five years and the father of your children that you may still love your former boyfriend? You know, the one who broke your heart and nearly killed your spirit? The one who left you like Tamar? That one. And for a split second I thought about lying—if I denied it, I would spare Randy the gory details and not hurt him. But then I thought twice about it. *He'll know*, I thought to myself. *He always knows.*

He turned the car off and shifted himself to the right so he could see me. Reaching for my hand he said, "Kelly, look at me."

I felt the sting of water fill my eyes before the blur ever came. I didn't want him to know; he had been too good to me. He continued, "Listen to me," turning his head and oddly looking up so I couldn't do anything but look at him. Rubbing his thumbs over the top of my knuckles, he paused, then just above a whisper said, "If you still love him, we need to find that out, okay?"

"But..."

"No 'buts'...we'll figure it out. Let's just go on Saturday and meet him...and we'll take it from there."

There was the Light. Exposing everything, all without making me feel dirty or condemned. I sat back, blown away by his reaction. "How do you do that?"

"Do what?" he asked.

"How do you remove yourself like it doesn't matter?"

His immediate response to my question has become, over time, a fundamental principle in successful communication for both of us throughout our marriage. He simply said, "Kelly, loving someone is about becoming what they need you to be—it's about learning what hat to wear. Right now, I need to be your friend, not your husband."

He paused again, then looked at me and continued, "Don't misunderstand... I'm not crazy about the situation, but this isn't about me. It's about Matthew ...and it's about you making peace with your past. I love you...and it *is* going to be okay. I trust that."

I stared at him, unable to shift my gaze. His words were like a lamp that exposed my darkness—those places where for weeks I had been tormented by fear and shame about the possibility of former feelings. Instantly I felt the desire to come out of hiding as courage began to strengthen my resolve. I felt myself being drawn to the freedom the spoken words represented, and within minutes I felt the grip of Shame begin to ease as the warmth of the Light penetrated my soul. Freedom reigned out in the open, and I found myself once again like Eve after the Fall—beginning to emerge from my own hiding place in search of freedom from my shame.

As if that conversation wasn't enough Randy led the way throughout that whole experience, and I watched him that following Saturday morning as he skillfully and graciously extended mercy to a man who could have posed a viable threat to Randy's family and marriage but, in the end, didn't. Rather, throughout our twenty plus years of marriage Randy's selflessness and commitment to abiding in the Truth has played an ongoing and vital role in exposing our silent tormentors and setting the captives free.

CHAPTER THIRTY-FiVE

Clarifying Miracles

Therefore do not be like them. For your Father knows the
things you have need of before you ask Him.

Matthew 6:8

WITHIN TWO YEARS of moving to the new house or what
the Lord would ultimately define as my own "Egypt" or
personal land of captivity, our overall circumstances began to
radically deteriorate to the point of near destruction. Although
relationally Randy and I had become inseparable, Matthew's
school environment became increasingly challenging during
third grade due to pornography in another student's backpack
and sexually permissive books being shared on the school bus.
Despite our continued efforts to rectify the situation the school
officials refused to take any action. Each offense seemed to
cement my feeling that Matthew's innocence was gradually
being eroded by a force I had little control over, contributing to

my belief that had I remained in my former community I could have effectively intervened on his behalf. But here each of our failed efforts ultimately served as reminders of the cost others would pay for my own disobedience.

In addition to the school issue was the consistent financial pressure we lived under. For the past 18 months we had been paying both a first and second mortgage, and Randy was bearing the full responsibility of providing for a family of five. We frequently entertained the thought of my returning to work as a way to ease the pressure, but analytically speaking we realized I would be working only to pay daycare; besides neither of us could dismiss the reoccurring sense that my working would somehow take the issue out of God's hands. It was as if the situation that lay at our feet was really a choice— we could either solve our dilemma in the natural and lose our spiritual advantage, or we could choose to be like Shadrach, Meshach and Abed-Nego (Daniel 3:19-25) and willingly stay in our own personal fiery furnace even though we didn't fully understand or see exactly how we would prevail.

By summer things had hit an all time low. Despite Randy working two different jobs it was as if something had pulled the plug on our finances and no matter how he tried to make ends meet or how much money he brought in, it was never enough. There didn't seem to be a blessing on the fruit of his labor, and although we cut every corner we knew to eliminate, it wasn't long before he resorted to selling pieces of his basketball card collection to buy food.

These were the days when we would try and apply scriptural truth in every way we knew how. Over and over we would recite, *"Trust in the LORD with all your heart, lean not on your own understanding; in all your ways acknowledge Him, and He shall direct your paths"* (Proverbs 3:5), as a way of both asking and trying to believe He would show us how to navigate through our situation. And every time we sunk deeper into the pit of despair, we questioned if we had given him the "all" part of our heart. Like the theology of Job's friends, we believed there had to be something we obviously weren't doing, otherwise why would this be happening?

Spinning our wheels, we felt the rut of our spiritual despair digging deeper, which caused us to try harder with the Lord and Randy to work longer hours in hopes of turning the course of our circumstances. All of it was to no avail.

By the end of summer we could no longer afford to pay our car insurance, and I remember the conversation with our agent as he tried to convince me otherwise, "Kelly, you have to have car insurance; it's the law."

Completely frustrated and humiliated by my situation, I curtly responded, "I know, but it's either I pay my house payment or live in my insured car. What would you recommend?"

I'm not sure if he was stunned by my rudeness or the direness of my situation; I just remember he quietly conceded to my argument and hung up the phone. Desperation had taken over—I never saw myself as one of "those people" who couldn't afford their car insurance or their food. *Where are you, Lord? I don't understand...* coursed through my mind.

I went through my mental checklist of requirements ... Tithe, check. Devotional time, check. Volunteer, check. *What do You want from me?* I asked Him.

Silence was the only response, which incited my frustration and anger, as well as arousing my self righteousness. Again,

I rattled off my checklist of required acts of obedience. *I've done everything You've asked—what more do You want?* For a second time silence filled the air. I watched the kids laugh as they played on the floor, oblivious to our plot in life, and I either envied or resented their ignorance—I wasn't sure which. I couldn't help but think about the people I knew… family, friends…*no one else seems to be struggling. Why are we?*

The agitation from my unanswered questions began to rise. I leaned across the counter and continued to watch the kids as if their play held some mysterious answer to my questions. *I don't understand, Lord. We've done all that we can—what are we missing?*

Beyond the laughter of my children the room remained eerily silent and it struck me how the Lord goes oddly quiet when He's already said everything He needs to say on a certain subject; the only thing He really requires is for us to rely on His truth. Admittedly, leaning on that counter I was as confused and frustrated as anyone could be. Situations like that are hard enough when you aren't a person of faith. But when you are and you act out of a place of obedience, believing God for who He says He is, and He doesn't "show up" when it looks and feels like He should—not only do you have the original circumstance to contend with, you also have a faith crisis on your hands.

In that moment, Randy and I believed we had applied and walked out the Truth in every way we knew how, but what we couldn't see was that our focus, just like the house, was on us. We didn't understand that it wasn't up to us to *do* anything— what He was wanting was for us to learn how to have an abiding reliance on Him. The very things I was using as a defense or as a case for Him to move on our behalf were the very things He was trying to break off: performance, earned favor, self righteousness, and religion. God doesn't move on our behalf because we earn it; He moves on our behalf because He loves us. While He calls us to a life of obedience, it's His love for us and ours for Him that makes us *want* to obey—not a list of do's and don'ts that earn us our spot in His presence or make us a recipient of His provision.

So there I was still leaning on the counter, waiting for a "Thus sayeth the Lord" moment from God when I decided that I was getting nowhere fast and leaned over to flip on the radio. It was 10 a.m. and Mike McIntosh was due to come on with his daily sermon. As I started to sort the mail, something Mike said bounced off the walls until it landed in the center of my spirit.

He referenced the Israelites and read a passage from Exodus 16 when God fed the Israelites with manna from heaven, and as my children played at my feet I began to take in the truth of what Mike was preaching. God's command to the Israelites was to, *"Let every man gather it according to each one's need, one omer for each person, according to the number of persons; let every man take for those who are in his tent"* (Exodus 16:16), then further in Exodus 16:20, *"Notwithstanding they did not heed Moses. But some of them left part of it until morning, and it bred worms and stank. And Moses was angry with them."*

Hearing from the Lord is often like listening from underwater. I immediately knew the Lord was trying to respond to my earlier inquiries but I couldn't fully understand Him so I asked, *What is it, Lord? What are You saying to me?*

225

Mike went on to explain that the Lord supernaturally provided for the Israelites on a daily basis and that they could only take what they needed for the members of their tent daily; they were not to store up nor worry about tomorrow. They were called to live in complete reliance and dependency on God and His provision if they were to survive in the wilderness.

I stood still trying to absorb the Truth of what I had just heard. Because the Lord had already shown me that I had sold myself into captivity when I bought the house, I could accept that He was in the process of delivering me to the Promised Land. *So is this my wilderness, Lord?* I asked. If so, then what Mike was saying about the provision of manna and the other spiritual principles that were embedded in the Exodus story were spiritual navigational points for my soul.

I ran to get my journal and began to pen down what I believed the Lord was writing on my heart:

1) God's heart is for me to rely upon Him for my every need,

2) God *will* provide for my family on a daily basis, and

3) I am not to store up nor rely upon any other source of nourishment; my eyes are to be fixed on His provision alone.

I reread what the Lord had shown me and stood in awe at the timing of His word. It all sounded wonderful, but I deeply questioned my ability to actually live according to what He had just spoken; I had so much fear and it sounded so much easier said than done. *How do I do this, Lord, when I don't even have milk for my kids?* I asked.

"Just ask Me, Kelly. Teach them to ask Me."

As if I was learning how to walk all over again, I struggled to find the courage to let go of the counter and take my first step toward my goal. I released my grip and stood there, teetering on my spiritual feet, afraid of falling for I wasn't sure where I would land. *What if this doesn't work?* I silently questioned.

"*Then you're no worse off than when you started, are you?*"

I leaned over to turn the radio off and tentatively knelt down by my kids on the floor. "Hey guys, what are you doing?"

Aaron, always my cuddler, quickly scrambled his way up to my lap. "Nothin,' Mom." Matt answered, "Just trying to build something."

Clearing my throat, I hesitated then asked, "Do you guys want to pray with me?"

Anna jumped in, "I do. I wanna pray."

I was struck again by their complete trust. "How about we ask God for our food today? Would that be okay?"

Matt, old enough to be aware of the situation and always acutely aware to the things of the Spirit said, "We need to Mom. We don't have any milk."

"Well...then let's ask."

And there we sat, my three children and me in the middle of our kitchen floor, heads bowed and hands held asking our Father for food that we didn't have money to buy. Countless years later, I'm still not sure I am fully aware of everything God did that morning with regards to the formation of their faith, or mine, but I do know that after we said amen and decided to go for a walk, my circumstances weren't quite so overwhelming. And after we enjoyed the wagon ride and decided to turn back toward our home in the middle of that cul-de-sac, words cannot express the impact that came from seeing our porch overflowing with boxes and boxes of food and more milk than our refrigerator could hold.

CHAPTER THIRTY-SIX

"I Just Didn't Know..."

Most assuredly I say to you, we speak what we know
and testify what we have seen...
John 3:11

THE LORD'S PROVISION continued to sporadically manifest
in our lives in similar ways over the course of the next year.
Certainly we remained financially behind the eight ball
and the pressure never let up for very long, but through the
difficulties our faith was strengthened and we walked on new
heights, despite our dismal circumstances. It was during that
season, what St. John of the Cross calls the "Dark Night of
the Soul," when our spiritual foundation was securely laid and
true aspects of the character of God were permanently etched
in our souls.

Two pivotal financial principles that came out of the
Exodus experience and have governed our life since those

early days are simply:

1) We have what we need for today, and

2) Live wisely for today and trust God for tomorrow.

More times than not, when finances continue to ebb and flow, we have to repeatedly remind ourselves of these two governing principles, and their resounding truth somehow speaks into the world of chaos that "lack" threatens to create.

It wasn't long after the miraculous food event that the Lord began to broaden my volunteer efforts by introducing me to a new organization that taught abstinence in the public schools. While I didn't have a complete language for the havoc my teenage choices brought to my life, I knew my life's story brought credibility and practical support to the idea of waiting until marriage, thereby making my involvement fairly certain.

It's interesting to me how our inner man learns to function without being entirely intact, just as our physical bodies learn to compensate and adapt when a limb or sensory organ is no longer there or fully functional. For example, when one is born or becomes deaf or blind, the remaining four senses become greater as a way to compensate for the "deficit." So it is with our inner man—when we become violated or wounded and a piece of ourselves is no longer healthy, our spirits overcompensate and we learn coping mechanisms to try to function as normally as possible until we no longer remember what life was like prior to the wounding.

For me, it had been nearly ten years since the events in Ohio occurred and I had, for the most part, learned to employ my own set of coping skills that allowed me to function "normally." I still found most of my solace in a tightly protected social world, and Randy remained my shield and body guard when entering unfamiliar places. I still didn't venture too far out of my bubble for fear of the unknown, yet when required, had learned to effectively compensate my way through new and uncharted territories.

It was mid fall when the teacher's training for the abstinence program began, and it took everything I had to muster up the courage to go by myself. Somehow as I drove to the director's house, Rejection had slithered its way into my car and by the time I pulled in the driveway it had nearly convinced me I wasn't welcome and that I was completely out of place: "You don't belong here, you know? They won't like you."

I tried to argue against its stream of logic but knew from past experience how much I hated the feeling of standing out against the crowd, of being different, which gave way to another onslaught, "You're not going to fit in—you never do." Fighting to find some kind of common ground to walk on, I looked through my windshield and was overwhelmed by the enormity of the house. "See, they're going to know; look at how wealthy they are and you....you don't have anything. They'll know, you won't be able to hide it. Don't go in there... just leave, no one will even know you were here."

I sat frozen as I watched numerous women, all of whom I didn't know, get out of their cars. They appeared happy, content within themselves, and I coveted their freedom. "I can't go in there," I whispered to myself, "I don't even know what to say." I turned to the left and reached for my seatbelt, fully intending to leave but nearly screamed at the sight of my Crisis Pregnancy Center director standing at my car door smiling and waving at me.

Rolling the window down I asked her, "What are you doing here? I didn't know you were coming."

"Just thought I'd check it out since we've been marketing it through the Center," she answered. Then looking at me with the same probing eyes as Randy's, she asked, "You okay?"

Aware for the first time that Rejection had grown silent, I quickly answered, "Yeah..yeah...I'm fine," and began gathering my things to get out of the car.

We walked into the lower level great room filled with nearly twenty women, all of who seemed to know one another; petrified, I stuck like glue to my director. Scanning the room, I took in the finishing details of fine wood and an enormous fireplace across from a full bar. *My whole house could fit into this one room*, I thought to myself. Behind me stood the pool table and straight ahead was a video setup where the actual training would occur.

Milling about the room were the women clustered in their own familiar groups as I did my best to melt into the wall. I tried to smile or nod when one of them looked at me while my insides flipped every which way but straight. I would have much rather screamed, "I don't belong here," and turned around and run out, but my feet felt like they were set in cement; I couldn't go anywhere—not in, not out, nowhere. It wasn't long before my director friend guided me like a little old lady to a nearby chair and said, "Why don't you sit down, Kelly. You don't look so good."

I sat tormented by my own plaguing fears and silently wondered what in the world was wrong with me. Finally the director of the program started her introduction and went on to explain the organization's mission was to equip teenagers with the goal of abstinence. Then she supported the idea with the most recent statistics on teenage pregnancy, STDs and abortion, all of which were cause for immediate intervention. As she finished her presentation and introduced the video, the lights started to fade and I sat back relishing the opportunity to finally morph into the dimness of my surroundings.

As the screen went black I reflected on the fact that I was one of those "statistics" she had cited. Then I wondered if life would have been different had I sat through an abstinence class. *Would I have been able to say no?*

The hush of the room filled the air as the video started by documenting the evolution of the sexual revolution and how much we as a society have adapted our way of thinking to fit the social norms. Then a young girl of approximately 17 appeared on the video and began telling her story, how she had always believed in waiting until she was married but somehow things changed when she met this one boy. She believed she loved him.

I was glued—oblivious to anyone else in the room. I knew this girl was somehow telling my story but with her words, giving me a language so I could understand what had been left so unresolved in my spirit. I leaned forward in my chair as if I was physically pressing into what she was saying.

"…They all make it look so easy, but it's not. They make it look like it's no big deal. No one told me…no one ever told me I would feel this way afterwards."

Her tears came as the reporter asked, "How did you feel?"

"Broken. Like a huge hole had been left in the middle of my heart…like a huge piece of me had been left behind." She paused to catch her breath. "If I had known I was giving so much more than just my physical body, I would have chosen differently. No one ever told me." And the screen faded to black.

I sat back, closed my eyes and told myself, *That's me... that's exactly how I feel. No one ever told me I wouldn't be the same.* It was like an epiphany and suddenly memories of the mornings when I would wake up being thankful for my virginity despite pushing the limits consumed my mind. I silently sought the Lord, *Is this what You were trying to prevent—this feeling of regret? Of sorrow?* I tried to listen for an answer but continued, *Is this what You were trying to tell me?*

I struggled to focus as the director came back to the front, but remained lost in my own thoughts. I conducted a mental tally of how I felt:

1) *What exactly do I regret? Was it Matthew?*
   No—he was the best thing that came out of the situation.

2) *Was it the relationship itself?*
   Admittedly, I had to really think about that—I deeply regretted my involvement with a married man and felt terrible for whatever part I played in the demise of his marriage, but thankful that I had Matthew.

3) *Giving myself to him?*

I sat and tried to remember how I felt the morning after, and let my mind go back to the events of ten years ago. I thought about the trite dismissal I struggled to apply to the situation, and how I immediately tried to convince myself that it was what some of my friends had described as "no big deal," but I instinctively knew better. I remembered seeing my heart scattered across the highway as I left Ohio for the last time and knew that if I had held the line and said no, my heart would still be largely in one piece.

The final memory that coursed through my mind was the moment of my crying out in the car that "I didn't know—I didn't know how much pain it would bring," which brought me full circle back to my present moment and the other 17-year-old girl who was distraught with regret for doing something that had profoundly deep and unexpected consequences.

I opened my eyes and shook my head as if I was waking up from a dream. Now what, Lord? I silently whispered, neither of us knew, but what now?

"*You tell them—it's part of your story.*"

"Lord, I can't even walk into a room of strangers; how am I ever going to speak to them?"

"*My people are destroyed for lack of knowledge*" (Hosea 4:6). Then silence.

I thought about my own destruction and wondered how many young girls would be spared if the truth were really told. Would I have been spared?

Truthfully, I'll never know but I can't say it keeps me from wondering...and at the end of my wonderment I always come full circle to the knowledge that I serve a sovereign God who has a sovereign way about Him and, for whatever reason He deems necessary, He repeatedly chooses to confound the wise with the foolish and has proven Himself more than faithful to turn my ashes into something amazingly and profoundly beautiful.

And most days, that's all I need to know.

CHAPTER THIRTY-SEVEN

Preparing to Leave Egypt

For I know that my Redeemer lives,
And He shall stand at last on the earth;
And after my skin is destroyed, this I know,
That in my flesh I shall see God.
Job 19:25-26

As for most people, the mark of a new year brought for us the anticipation and hope that things would begin to turn around for our family. We had financially weathered Christmas with unexpected help from our own "secret Santa" who anonymously and abundantly gave Christmas gifts to our children, once again confirming the Scripture that He knows our need before we even ask.

Yet by February, things were becoming dire and we were feeling forced to do something to stay afloat. We had already eliminated as many unnecessary expenses as possible and didn't see any other tangible areas to cut. The only solution that seemed viable was to refinance the house, thereby reducing our payment by extending the term and increasing our monthly cash flow. On the surface it seemed completely logical yet something within my spirit remained resistant to the idea. I immediately connected the dots and knew that if we went through with the refinance we were indirectly choosing to stay in that house, and that thought tormented me. I didn't want to live in my captivity one day longer than necessary.

Subsequently I found my spirit continually crying out to the Lord, *Please, please don't let this happen—do something.* But silence was His ongoing response. I resorted once again to begging and pleading with Randy to reconsider, but the numbers were the numbers, and we weren't making it. Something had to change.

By the end of February, Randy had made all the necessary arrangements and had put the ball in motion for the refinancing to occur. Marking my desperation, I increased my petitions to the Lord. I fully understood our financial predicament but the ongoing sense that we didn't belong there wouldn't leave me alone. It was as if every time I crossed the invisible line that marked the boundary between the area we currently lived and the one where Randy and I first started out, an overwhelming sense that I was home would envelop me. It felt like I was being beckoned or called back by an unseen force, which always resulted in my questioning, *But Lord, how do I reconcile our circumstances with this feeling? Is this You trying to tell me something?*

Frantic to ease my conflict, I made countless trips driving up and down various streets in my former community searching for the one house the Lord would make available. I endlessly drove through all four districts of the community until I finally resorted to negotiating with the Lord, *I'll make this one work*, or *Lord, if you do this I'll never*..... whatever it took to fill in the blank. I was desperate to be out from under my self-inflicted yoke of bondage. So much so that when the doors back to my beloved community refused to open, I began entertaining the thought that maybe I was too narrow-minded in my search. Therefore, in an effort to demonstrate flexibility, I began to present Him with various options: *What do you think, Lord, city or country? Big house or little? Thriving, upcoming area or where I used to live?* Exhausted, I finally cried out, *Lord, I'll go anywhere, just not here—I'm sorry!!*

Once again, Silence was the only response, which propelled me into further confusion. I literally had no clue or vision as to what God was doing; I just knew I wanted out—out from my torment and out of that house. I spent hours searching the Scriptures and the one that always caught my attention was Psalm 46:10, "Be still and know that I am God," or as New American Standard translates it, "Cease striving and know that I am God."

Every time I read that verse it seemed as if, in the moment, my mind could grasp the peace that the command "Be still" represented, but no matter how I fought, my spirit couldn't hold onto it. I would ask the Lord to make me still, but no sooner would I sit and try to meditate on the verse then life would call my name and I would feel my striving begin all over again. No matter how I tried it seemed like the peace that came from the Truth always remained more on the page than it ever did in my soul.

The possibility of escaping the pressure of our circumstances was useless. The reality was I lived in a home that not only I didn't want and couldn't afford, causing other bills to mount up with no way to pay them, but I felt called to be part of a community where I no longer lived. In essence, the Lord had hemmed us in on all sides or as the apostle Paul says, "We are hard pressed on every side, yet not crushed; we are perplexed, but not in despair; persecuted, but not forsaken; struck down, but not destroyed" (2 Cor. 4:8).

The only way out of our mess appeared to be through refinancing and though my heart was sickened by the thought, I was more committed to not repeating the mistakes of my first rebellion so I submitted to Randy's plan.

It was late February and Randy had an appointment with the loan officer on the same morning I was scheduled to teach abstinence at a nearby school. Grasping my last ray of hope, I reminded Randy of our spiritual hesitation to stay in the house, earnestly seeking some kind of physical reaction that would indicate his apprehension. But there was nothing. I looked outside and watched as the snowflakes fell, silently wondering if what Randy was about to do was really God's heart for us. "I don't know what to do with this sense of foreboding that rises up in me every time we actually contemplate this course of action. Where do I put that?" I asked him.

He turned to look at me, paused, then said, "All we can do, Kelly, is ask God to shut the door if He doesn't want us to walk through it."

"I have been," I replied, the desperation in my voice betraying my calm veneer. "So unless the door shuts this morning, you're going to walk through it?" I asked.

His eyes locked with mine and I knew his answer, and couldn't help but wonder if he felt the same sense of dread I did. If not, then one of us is wrong, I told myself—*We're always in unity.*

I wrestled with the remnants of our conversation as I drove to the babysitter's and found myself doing exactly what Randy had indirectly instructed—I offered up as many prayers as I could muster, begging the Lord to close the door if we were outside of His will. *I don't know what You want here, Lord, but I know I'm not at peace with this. If this isn't You, then please shut whatever doors you don't want Randy walking through. Please prevent him from making the appointment this morning.*

Over and over I recited that prayer or something like it—so much so that by the time I pulled into the babysitter's driveway I was a nervous mess. The thought of being outside of God's will terrified me for I had been living in that place for nearly three years; I couldn't get my head around possibly having to do it for the unforeseeable future.

In hopes of hearing something from the Lord, I waited for as long as I could before I corralled both the kids out of the car then worked our way through the newly fallen snow toward the front step. Giggles and the sound of a TV announcer seeped through the crack of the door already ajar as I heard Elizabeth holler, "Come in!"

The entryway was full of little shoes and boots, and strewn across the parquet floor were various rags soaked from their efforts of absorbing the residual water left by the melted snow. I smiled as I walked in and nodded a silent hello to a man I had never met before. "Do you know David, Kelly? His parents live on Christopher Street," Elizabeth mediated.

"No, I'm sorry I don't. What's your last name?" I asked him.

He answered and I knew immediately who he was speaking of because his parents had frequently attended the ballgames Matthew played in, hoping to see their own grandson. "Yeah, I do know your parents. They're wonderful people," I said.

"They are, thank you. Do you live near them?" he asked.

"I did ... we moved a couple of years ago."

"Oh, well, they're selling their house so if you know of anyone who may be interested, would you let them know?" David said.

Stunned, I smiled and coughed out a broken, "Sure." I looked around the room as if an explanation could be found written on a wall or lingering in the air when my internal conversation began, *Wow, Lord!....really? What am I supposed to do with that?*

Kneeling down to uncloak my kids, I willed myself to hold it together, then kissed them goodbye and told Elizabeth I'd be back later. Walking back to the car I couldn't help but be struck by the unbelievable timing of the whole conversation. *We're in no place to do anything, Lord. I don't understand,* I told Him as I tried to avoid slipping off the road. *I don't know what's worse, not being able to find a house or to know of a house we would love to have, but not be in a position to get it. What do you want from me?* I cried out.

I was frustrated, perplexed and trying desperately to remain calm. Although our spirits felt like we were at war with what we were being "forced" to do, our physical circumstances seemed to necessitate our every move. *We won't survive our current situation, Lord. Please shut the door that no man can*

242

open and open the door that no man can close (Rev. 3:7) I begged.

It was the last prayer I uttered before spending most of the day at school teaching. Not until later that afternoon as I drove back from school and headed toward Elizabeth's to pick up my kids did I have the drive time to wonder what Randy would have said about that morning's news. *Would it have been his "closed door," Lord?* I asked.

"Be anxious in nothing, but in everything, by prayer and supplication, with thanksgiving, let your requests be made known to God" (Phil. 4:6) seemed to ricochet through the car. Tempted to argue the point that I had been praying and supplicating to what felt like no avail, I chose instead to remain silent and savor the quiet moment.

My preoccupied thoughts kept me company the entire way home, and it wasn't until I checked in with Randy later that afternoon that I discovered how the Lord had intervened in the day's events. Anxious to share with him the details about the house that David told me about, as soon as I got the three kids situated with their afternoon snacks I called Randy. Hearing the unusual tone of his voice distracted me from my mission and caused me to immediately ask him if he was okay. Without answering the question, he instantly began to explain, "Okay, when I left this morning I knew that we both were a bit hesitant about what to do so I began to ask the Lord to shut the door if refinancing wasn't what He wanted. It wasn't but a short time later the car started slowing down in the middle of the highway and no matter how hard I pushed the gas pedal, it wouldn't go any faster."

Silenced by impatient curiosity I mentally willed him to

continue. "Thankfully, I got the car on the shoulder before it died but no matter what I did, it wouldn't start again. I ended up walking to a gas station. The car's dead, Kelly."

"What do you mean? Who's fixing it?"

"That's exactly what I mean—it's not fixable. It's dead. The engine froze up."

"Oh," always one to quickly assimilate information, I was afraid to sound too excited. I strategically paused before asking, "Now what?"

I heard him exhale and pictured his face as his mind collected his words. "Well, we'll be down to one car until things turn around and …" he stopped.

I fought to keep from finishing his sentence. "Because of the car, Kel, I didn't make the appointment at the bank."

A holy moment of silence coursed through the phone lines as we both tried to understand the real meaning behind what had occurred that morning. After a few seconds he suggested, "Perhaps this is what we prayed for—maybe this was our closed door."

I became aware of holding my breath only after I heard my exhale. "I didn't see this coming, Randy. I'm not sure what to say," was all I could muster. I felt stunned and rendered speechless—more by the timing of the day's events than by the events themselves. *Anyone's car can break down, but today, Lord? I silently wondered, How does this happen?*

With Randy's account of the day left to hang in the balance, we agreed to talk later and hung up the phones. I leaned on the counter and watched my children enjoying one another's company, and thought about whether or not the timing of our prayers and the events of that day could be coincidental.

Are there such things as coincidences? I wondered, then entertained how peculiar it is that "coincidences" always seem to occur more frequently when prayer is involved.

"Well, if they're not coincidental then they must be sovereign," I whispered as the realization washed over me. One hundred thoughts crowded my mind until finally only the simplest remained: *Those events could be nothing less than a sovereign act of a sovereign God, a God who had heard the cries of His children and remained faithful to meet us in the midst of our newest and most profound need.*

Pushing myself off the counter, I walked over to my children, relishing the thought of God's intervention. I wanted them to know about the God they served, about His faithfulness and the way He worked. And although I failed to understand exactly where the events of that cold, snowy February morning would take us, I never imagined it would be into one of the most foundational and pivotal seasons of our lives.

CHAPTER THIRTY-EIGHT

Spying out
the Promised Land

Whoever comes to Me, and hears My sayings and does
them, I will show you whom he is like: He is like a man
building a house, who dug deep and laid the foundation
on the rock. And when the flood arose, the stream beat
vehemently against that house, and could not shake it,
for it was founded on the rock.
Luke 6:47-48

THE EVENTS OF the next four months would culminate in the
manifestation of God's heart for His children in significant and
unbelievable ways. It is because of the time spent in "Egypt"
that I learned the foundational spiritual principles that have
since governed my life. It was also during those days that I
grew to understand on a deeper level what the Lord means
when He says in Deuteronomy 4:29, "But from there you will

247

seek the LORD your God, and you will find Him if you seek Him with all your heart and with all your soul."

There is so much more to seeking God than just going to church and living "right." According to Jesus in the gospel of Luke it includes coming to Him, hearing Him and doing what He says. For me, that obedience began with actively seeking God from the place of my brokenness and despair; I only became serious about searching for God when I had nowhere else to turn because He had allowed my circumstances to hem me in. It was in that place of desperation when I actually stopped and allowed the Holy Spirit to finally "Search me, O God, and know my heart; try me, and know my anxieties; and see if there is any wicked way in me, and lead me in the way everlasting" (Psalm 139:23-24).

Only in that place of examination does one become real and authentic before a Holy God and our humanity cries out, "Woe is me, for I am undone!" (Isaiah 6:1). It was in that place that the depth of my rebellion became so abundantly apparent that I could do nothing but repent and cry out for this redemption. Only then did I become like Abram who with no other solution had to step outside of his circumstances and "look now toward heaven…" In other words, I had been taken, in one aspect, to the end of myself.

Although I was learning to seek the Lord continually, there were often times I wrestled with the need to have or demand answers to the things that didn't make sense. For example, I desperately fought to understand why after six weeks of negotiating for the house that David mentioned when I was at Elizabeth's, the sellers decided not to move. It had seemed completely logical to interpret the events of that morning as the Lord, so why wouldn't He want us to have that house? He was the One who had informed us about it—I hadn't fully grasped that God doesn't like to be put in a box, no matter how big it may be, and that His primary focus was for me to learn how to rest in His presence, not His provision.

Therefore, because of what was happening in the natural—falling behind in our mortgage, having only one car and mounting medical bills—I was gradually learning how God was allowing and using those things to draw me closer to Him. This season was about trusting and learning to lean on His faithfulness. I often felt as if I was being confronted with the choice to either have the spirit of Joshua and believe that God was going to deliver me *completely*, or be found like the Israelites who would grumble and complain about what deliverance looked like, ultimately begging to go back to my captivity where the routine was predictable because it was so familiar.

For whatever reason, God chose to give me the faith to believe in His deliverance. Undoubtedly I drew strength and reinforcement from Randy's unwavering belief that "... the LORD God will help Me; therefore I will not be disgraced; therefore I have set My face like a flint, and I know I will not be ashamed" (Isaiah 50:7). He was confident that the Lord said he could sell the house, therefore Randy became immovable. I watched as he reflected on his earlier acts of disobedience and recommitted to the Lord to do it His way, then marveled at how he had set his face toward doing it the way God wanted it done.

Sometimes it felt as if scenes were being reenacted all over again. As I watched him pound the stake into the ground one early March morning just as he had nearly three years ago, I wondered with bated breath what God had in store for us. I knew obedience required us to try to sell this house "by owner" just as we had our first home, but I was still struck by Randy's conviction when he told the neighbors, "God doesn't even need a sign in the yard if He wants this house sold. But I swear this For Sale by Owner sign is the only one that you will see in this yard."

And despite not having another home to purchase, we began showing the house to whomever was interested, and with every appointment I found myself waiting and watching to see if this was the day God would deliver us. Weeks went by, and inevitably each potential buyer would say something like, "Your house is lovely. Be patient, it will sell," and like a rollercoaster my emotions would rise and fall with every appointment. It wasn't until that phrase had been repeated over and over that we began to develop ears to hear and finally recognize it as a prophetic message from the Lord sent to strengthen and encourage us in the midst of our deteriorating circumstances.

With every passing week Randy and I were falling further and further behind financially and, while I was elated at the thought of moving, the reality was I still didn't know exactly what we could afford or where we would go—those were "things" I wasn't supposed to be anxious about. Still, I spent a fair amount of time convincing myself that my numerous tours through my former community were just me "knocking on the door." I never saw them as nurturing my idol, until one day Randy addressed their effect: "You need to let this go, Kel, it's consuming you."

"I know...I just don't know how."

He looked at me, and in a grace filled moment simply said, "For now, draw a boundary line around yourself. Don't go over there and don't ask anyone about moving—let's see if that helps."

I knew he was right, but in some regard it felt as if agreeing to his plan made the idea of moving back remote and unobtainable. I looked down and was again confronted with a choice—I could listen to Randy's wisdom and establish some sense of stability, or I could continue my self-inflicted torment of daily drive-throughs that felt like riding a rollercoaster without enough padding. I felt tossed around and suddenly very tired; freedom was within my grasp and I knew all I needed to do was choose. My eyes traced the pattern on the floor as I prayed for the strength to lay down my dream and said, "Okay, I'll stop."

By the time June approached, numerous people had come through the house but still no buyers. The house had been for sale just over three months when an old friend from our former community called to tell us a house had just become available by owner in the same district where we had once lived. Intent on maintaining my newly drawn boundary line, I politely listened as she recited the details of the house, then thanked her for calling and hung up, dismissing the information since we didn't have a buyer.

A few days later, the phone rang again—same friend, same information. This time she asked me if I had called on the house, which I admitted I hadn't so she pressed, "Oh, Kelly, it's really nice... you need to at least look at it."

Again, I thanked her and hung up. This time, though

still committed to my boundary line, I at least presented the information to Randy, who reacted with the same concern, no buyer. Dismissal number two.

God used the third phone call to get my attention and something in me grew curious about the whole situation. For a second I entertained the possibility of this being a coincidence but then realized it felt more like a Godly pursuit, and a freedom to take a small step over the boundary line began to emerge.

As I drove across the invisible dividing line between the two communities, I giggled at the realization that I was becoming more like Joshua every day—"I feel like I've been commissioned to spy out the Promised Land, Lord," I told Him as I parked the car in front of the house. I looked around and was immediately struck by the fact that for as many times as I had driven through this neighborhood, I had never even heard of this particular street—small and quaint like its broader surroundings, nothing about it particularly stood out. I sat in the car and tried to assess what all the pursuit had been about. It was a small house on a small unknown street with an unusually small For Sale sign that stood maybe a foot above the ground in the front yard. "This house looks so small," I told the kids as I unbuckled Aaron from his car seat, "but let's go find out."

As I stood on the tile entryway flanked by my three children on my right and left, I silently absorbed the ambiance of the small burgundy living room and immediately felt as if I had entered a holy moment. It wasn't as if the house was grand or I heard angels singing, I just *knew* that if the Lord was going to move us, it would be to this house. It had everything we needed and wanted: four bedrooms, a master bathroom, full finished basement with a bonus room, and it was in the community we loved at a price point we could afford.

If it's possible to fall in love with a house, I did, and as much as I tried to be poker faced, my reaction was evident— my heart was racing, my palms were sweating and the look on my face was silently screaming, "I love it! I want it!" Now all I had to do was ask Randy to look at it and beg the Lord not to sell it.

We waited until the following Friday afternoon for Randy to look at the house, but it didn't take long before he had the same sense as the kids and me—if God was going to move us, it would be to this house. I stood and listened as he spent his time talking with the seller about options and price, and when the request for earnest money was presented, Randy's immediate response was to tell her he would have to pray about it. Everything in me wanted to squeeze his hand or pinch him in hopes of conveying my urgency in the matter; I knew all too well how difficult it was to find a four bedroom in this community, let alone one we could afford. *What is he thinking?* I wondered as I started to fidget, fighting the urge to tell him, "If earnest money is what she wants, then let's find a way to get it to her."

I continued to occupy my thoughts with physical distractions as Randy tried to explain that he wasn't prepared to move outside of God's will or timing, and then asked if he could have the weekend to pray about things before he got back to her. My eyes shot up at him and I wanted to scream, "The whole weekend?!? That's three days...THREE..." but the cautious whisper of *"Daughter..."* in my spirit kept my tongue silent.

Silence remained with us as we walked back to the car, and I watched Randy as he took one last quick assessment of the neighborhood. I stood on my side of the car, waiting and looking for some kind of indicator that would reveal his thoughts. Somewhere along the short walk from the door to the car I remembered that we had borrowed the earnest money to purchase our current home, then like a flash I thought about the déjà vu feeling I had as I watched him pound the For Sale sign in our yard just a few months ago. "It's like everything is on repeat," I blurted out.

"What do you mean?" he asked as he opened his car door.

"It's as if each circumstance we're facing now is similar to one that occurred when we sold the first house, but now each time it's as if He's waiting to see if we'll do it differently…"

"If we'll be obedient," Randy said, finishing the sentence.

I agreed then quickly dismissed the anxiety that arose when I thought about having to take three days to figure out what God would have us do. In all reality we had barely pulled away from the house before we realized that although we wanted the home, we wouldn't borrow the money to secure a deposit on it. We both knew that we were going to have to walk in a place of faith that if God wanted us to have that house, it wouldn't take borrowed earnest money to get it. I thought about our situation as Randy drove back home, and realized that this wasn't going to be as easy as it sounded. But the bigger part of me knew that if we wanted our freedom restored, this would be the second visible step of faith and obedience we would have to take.

We pulled in our driveway knowing full well the ramifications that would come from refusing to put earnest money down. That house was located in a prime real estate market and offered more space than most in the area so by choosing to not secure the house through a down-payment, we were laying the house down at His feet and choosing to believe God for who He says He is. Our only option was to take things back in our own hands and be disobedient to what He had called us to do, which for us was really no option at all.

As difficult as it was, it took most of the weekend before we were able to surrender the house to Him and tell the seller we were unable to secure it with a deposit. I listened as Randy explained that while we loved the home, we needed to trust and rest on God's timing and provision. Then I watched as he hung up the phone and felt like my dream of moving was circling in the wind like the white seeds of a dandelion that get blown around on a summer day. I closed my eyes and prayed, not knowing exactly where my dream would land; I just knew that the two things that mattered most to us besides our children— the selling of our home and our desire to purchase the new one—now rested completely in His hands.

Attempts to second guess our decision intermittently tormented us over the next three days as we examined and reexamined whether we had really heard from the Lord. On the evening of the third day, our phone rang and after introducing herself, the seller simply said, "Randy, I can't explain this but I was quite taken with your family and I want you all to have this house. I've decided to pull the sign from my yard and give you thirty days to sell your home."

Stunned by her offer Randy stood, jaw dropped and speechless. Waving me over to him, he stammered and stuttered until he finally said, "You understand my house isn't sold and I don't even have anyone interested, don't you?"

He turned the phone outward so I could hear her sweetly reply, "I understand that." Then as if she somehow knew we needed to hear it just one more time, she finished the conversation with, "Let's just be patient—I'm sure your house is lovely and I believe it will sell," then said goodbye.

CHAPTER THIRTY-NINE

Battling for the Inheritance

…being confident of this very thing, that He who
has begun a good work in you will complete it
until the day of Jesus Christ.
Philippians 1:6

I OFTEN WONDER what the course of my life would have
been had I not first encountered the Lord that February night
in Ohio so many years ago. How different would my life be if
I had made another choice? What if He had not given me the
faith to believe? Who would I be? As always, the "what ifs"
remain unanswerable, but of this one thing I am assured—that
cold winter night when I felt completely alone and forsaken
was the single largest turning point of my life, and at the risk
of being corny I'd have to say, "He had me at "Hello.""

I would be remiss not to admit that there have been
numerous times over the years since then when the temptation

257

to feel abandoned and forsaken hits me all over again and all I want to do is quit this walk of faith because it's just too hard. Yet every time, He reminds me of an earlier conversation that occurred between Jesus and Peter after so many had left because Jesus' teachings were just too difficult:

From that time many of His disciples went back and walked with Him no more. Then Jesus said to the twelve, "Do you also want to go away?" But Simon Peter answered Him, "Lord, to whom shall we go? You have the words of eternal life" John 6:68-69.

Every time I go through something more difficult than the last thing, I become more aware of how His love for me has really given me no choice. He alone holds all that I need or want from life. I have no other place to go but to Him.

So it was during the weeks that followed the seller's offer to hold her house for thirty days. At first, we were elated... rewarded for having actively placed our trust in Him. We started off with such confidence but as time passed and financially we neared certain destruction, our faith began to waiver and questions about God's character rose to the surface. I learned, and had to relearn, that the doubt that would surface about God and His heart for us during that time was what He was really after and trying to transform. With each passing day, I could feel my heart start to wane under the pressure of mounting bills and calls from creditors. I truly didn't understand why God's deliverance was so delayed and frequently questioned why He would lead us out of Egypt just to leave us in the wilderness.

As the thirty day mark rapidly approached we had nothing—no money and still no viable interest in anyone buying our house. What we did have was one car and the mounting pressure the calendar represented. Desperation was getting more and more challenging to ward off as we tried to fight "the good fight of faith" (1 Timothy 6:12), and I would often ask the Lord to give me eyes to see where He was bringing reinforcements.

The biggest momentary relief from the battle came the last Thursday of June when I was scheduled to help with an evening training for the local Crisis Pregnancy Center. It was something I had been doing periodically throughout the year, so both the director and fellow volunteers were sources of encouragement and comfort to me. The day held its normal routine as I prepared dinner and waited just long enough for Randy to get home before I left with the car.

My mind drifted as I drove downtown, praying about our last scheduled open house before having to make a final decision. There was one remaining weekend before our time allotment expired, and we both knew it was our last chance to bring people in for a low risk look at the house. I stopped at the intersection and filled the time waiting for the light to change by asking the Lord to honor the prayers of His people, then asked Him to help me accept His answer. That was the hardest prayer of all.

Seconds later I heard the screech of tires, and before I knew what was happening felt my head whip backwards and the seatbelt burn into my shoulder as another woman's car slammed into the back of mine, shoving me halfway into the intersection. Things went momentarily surreal as if I was more of an onlooker than an actual participant ... then as reality settled in on me, I began to look around and immediately wonder what had happened. I struggled to find a navigational point since the light was no longer visible above me. I looked around and slowly began to gain enough composure to realize I was okay.

I discovered as soon as I stepped out of the car that it was no longer driveable for the back tires were now buckled under the passenger bench, and simultaneously heard myself thank God that my children weren't in the car, then ask, *Now what are we going to do?* In the midst of the sirens and chaos, Silence seemed to find his way to the scene for I heard nothing and offered little to say other than to ask the officers to drive me home.

Only when I reached Randy did the adrenaline of the moment release me and the torrent of emotions come flooding out. "I don't understand… why is God doing this?" I cried out. "We've done everything He's asked, what more does He want?"

Randy just looked at me. "I don't know, Kel. I just know God isn't doing this."

"Well, He isn't doing anything to stop it," I retorted. I was angry, confused and worn out. I sat on the edge of the couch wanting to believe the way Randy did; I wanted to trust God's heart but the reality was I didn't. I felt punished somehow, as if I had missed something along the way that had angered Him and this was His discipline. "I just don't understand."

Randy slowly leaned forward and wrapped his hands around mine and prayed. He shared with the Lord his heart for his family and his heart to move. Then I heard his voice waver as he confessed we had nothing to offer but our brokenness. He spoke of our financial devastation and then confessed to the Lord that the only thing we really had left was our car and now that was gone. He asked the Lord to move on our behalf and to show Himself in a miraculous way, then thanked the Lord in advance for what He was going to do.

The last thing I heard Randy say was something like, "Not our will, but Yours" and that's when Peace washed over me. It was the peace that was outside of my understanding—the peace that went beyond our natural circumstances and permeated every part of my being and made me know that no matter what happened over the next three days, we were going to be okay. God would somehow take us from this place of wilderness into His Promised Land for He who had been faithful to begin the good work would be faithful to complete it. He promised.

CHAPTER FORTY

To Him and Him Alone

Now to Him who is able to do exceedingly abundantly
above all that we ask or think, according to the power that
works in us, to Him be glory in the church by Christ Jesus to
all generations, forever and ever. Amen.
Ephesians 3:20-21

I ENTERED THE final three days of our allotted time fighting
to hold onto the peace that had enveloped my soul Thursday
evening. After four months of having the house on the market
the phone had grown silent, and whatever initial interest
there was had fallen to an all time low. I tried willing the
phone to ring every time I walked past it, and despite all the
encouragement and signs along the way, I still couldn't find
myself able to fully rest on what appeared as firm indicators
that He would move us. I continued to deeply wrestle with
the idea that God's will may very well include us staying put,

and I dreaded the thought of having to reconcile all that had happened with actually accepting not moving.

If I allowed my mind to wander, the questions would pummel my soul: *Then why? Why would He let the car break down if He wasn't going to let us move?* It's funny how the questions were always more about God's character than they ever were about my actual situation. It was as if something was coming against me in hopes of crippling my infant belief in a good God. Somehow during all the waiting, the focus of the battle would vacillate from the actual housing situation to wrestling with the goodness and faithfulness of God.

I would often find myself, for no apparent reason, pondering the thought that if God was good then why are we in the middle of this dire situation? Hadn't we done everything He'd asked? There was never any audible answer, just my own internal wrestling matches that often threatened to strangle my faith. But inevitably just about the time I would start to sink under the pressure, the storm clouds would somehow break and I would feel a momentary reprieve from the inner assault.

With only the Saturday to prepare for our last official Open House scheduled for Sunday afternoon, Randy, the kids and I set to cleaning the house. We spent most of that weekend giving it our best and final effort knowing full well this was our own personal "D Day." Come Sunday the signs would be hung, the house groomed and the lawn manicured and the kids and I would escape to my mom's as Randy did what he could to sell the house. I think we both knew the situation was really out of our hands, and there was nothing we could do to really sell the house if God didn't want it sold. We were merely going through the motions.

As the 2 p.m. hour approached, the sun was peeking through the clouds and the house never looked better. Randy had just returned from posting the Open House signs, and as the kids and I prepared to leave, we all said one final prayer asking God to release us from our wilderness. Standing in our prayer circle none of us were ready or willing to move and break up the moment. "This is it," I said as I fought to keep my stomach in its cavity.

I felt like I was on a rollercoaster and the "tick tick tick" of the car was announcing my ascent to the top of the hill so that my palms were moist with sweat and my brain was commanding my voice to scream, "LET ME OUT, I DON'T WANT TO RIDE!!" but it didn't listen. So ride I do, and by the time the car squeals over the top of the ride, I'm airborne with only the shoulder harness keeping me secure and the one thing that comes out of my throat isn't my voice, but my stomach, which no longer resides below my lungs. I hate rollercoasters—they incite the worst kind of fear in me. Yep, that's exactly how I felt in that prayer circle; I was the mother, the one who was supposed to be the model of faith, and all I could really do was wipe my damp hands on my shorts, give a halfhearted smile to Randy while I swallowed my stomach, and take our kids to my mom's in an effort to get off the ride.

Supplied with a rental car, I pulled in my mother's driveway and noticed a sudden chill in the air and the smell of rain that blew across the driveway. "Hmm," I said, "I didn't think it was supposed to rain." I cocked my head and looked up—*Oh Lord, are you kidding me?* I asked as I took in the approaching thunder clouds. I closed my eyes understanding full well what rain meant to our house. We lived in the center of the cul-de-sac where everyone's backyard drained into a creek, but on torrential stormy days the creek would overflow and create a lake in the backyard. In pristine condition it was beautiful—on stormy days it turned into a muddy mess. This looked like it was going to be a muddy mess day.

An hour later my mother's house grew dark as the electricity flickered and the rain pounded the windows. "This isn't good," I told my mom as Matthew, Anna and I played Go Fish. Seconds later my mother's phone rang and she said, "Kelly, it's Randy—he'd like to talk to you."

"It's over, Kel … I'm sorry," he said.

"What do you mean?" I asked him.

He began to explain that during the first thirty or forty-five minutes things went fairly well. He had four or five people come through and it looked promising. However, by 4:00 or 4:15, the rain came down so heavily that both the backyard and the cul-de-sac had flooded. His tone conveyed his weariness as he said, "There was so much water, Kelly, I had to pull an elderly couple's car into the garage so they could leave without wading across the driveway."

The last thing he said before he was finished was that one of our neighbors called to say the signs had blown down. "We're done."

I blindly felt around for a chair to sit in as I struggled to make sense of all he had just said. It was clear without his explanation that none of the people who had looked at the house were serious buyers. "I don't know what to say, Randy."

"Just come home; I need to be with you and the kids."

By the time we said goodbye to my mother and I loaded the kids in the car, the rain had subsided and the sun was once again trying to peek through the clouds. I glanced down at the clock and registered the 4:45 p.m. time. Fighting to not let bitterness take root in my spirit, all I could mumble was a weak, *I don't understand* to the Lord.

Randy was standing outside with the neighbors, sign in hand, as I turned into the court. Seeing the yard without the sign made me feel as if I had been sucker punched by an unknown force. I sat, unable to face the inevitable interrogation from the neighbors, role playing different conversations in my head as the kids got out of the car, *Oh, so you're not moving*, or *Couldn't sell it by owner? We tried to tell you.*

I twirled my keys in my hand trying to swallow the ever growing lump in my throat and summoned all the courage I could in order to face my accusers.

There was an immediate lull in Randy's conversation as I approached the spontaneous gathering. I silently greeted each of them, internally begging them not to ask me anything. The wind had died down, leaving us with a gentle breeze that caused the thin metal of the sign to ripple as if it wasn't willing to let me forget it was the topic of conversation. I listened as Randy explained to them the events of the day and then stood shocked as one of them felt the need to ask, "Well, I'm not sure I understand. Didn't you say God didn't need a sign to sell this house? Where's your God now?"

My knees nearly buckled with the force of his words. For the first time since arriving home, I looked up and saw the torment of the past five months written on Randy's face as he struggled to find an answer. "I don't have an answer yet," he said, "but I know God is still good."

I closed my eyes and quietly turned around to search for

solace. I walked to the front step and sat down, watching the kids play basketball; the gentleness of their play struck me as Matthew took turns trying to lift Anna and Aaron so they could each make a shot. It wasn't long before Randy, still with his sign, came and without saying a word sat next to me. I laid my head on his shoulder and simply said, "I don't understand."

"I know," was his only response.

An indefinite amount of time passed as we sat there silently, until finally he added, "The only thing I hear, Kelly, is you have to die to this thing. You have to let go. Completely."

I felt the familiar sting of tears and admitted, "I don't know how."

"The Lord will show you."

He sat there for seconds longer before getting up to finally put the sign away. I wondered when he was planning on calling the seller of the other house to tell her we couldn't buy it. I figured he wasn't feeling a lot of incentive to move things along; he knew she didn't have plans to purchase anything herself, and it certainly wasn't going to be easy for him to concede the battle. I took a deep inhale as I tried to soak in my solitude. I saw myself trying to cross a finish line but felt as if no sooner did I get to the yellow ribbon that represented relief then the line would get moved. *I'm trying, Lord. I just don't know how much longer I can run.*

Later that night, after the two younger kids were in bed, Randy made his dreaded phone call. I chose to stay in the family room with Matt and watch a movie; I wasn't ready to play an active role in burying the dream that was barely dead. Brokenness, if you haven't been there, is a hard thing to explain. Brokenness doesn't leave you hopeless; you still hope but true brokenness occurs when you go through the process of finally letting go of what you believed you couldn't live without in order to hold onto the One thing that you can't actually see, but you know it's there.

Undoubtedly, we were broken. I could see it as Randy walked to join us in the family room. He didn't walk heavy but he walked a bit worn out, with his shoulders a bit slumped, as if he wasn't exactly sure where he was headed. "Well, I told her."

"Yeah, what'd she say?

"She was sorry we couldn't sell. But what can she do?"

He paused, then shared his thought about contacting the bank during the upcoming week to start the refinancing process. The unavoidable reality of the day was settling in on all of us and all I could do was try to silently encourage him. We were both speechless—at a loss for words and void of understanding. I traced the dots that covered the couch, allowing my eyes to see figures that didn't really exist.

Silence permeated the room despite the movie that was playing in the VCR. Acceptance of our lot in life was slowly coming, but we both knew that grieving had to occur. Didn't Job have to sit in the ashes of ruin and weep before God restored him? We would grieve for days at the thought of letting go of our dream, and I would grieve all over again for the cost of my disobedience. I knew I was forgiven but I couldn't help but believe this was a refresher course for learning that even forgiven sins have consequences.

Our sleep that night was unsettling as we fought to accept the Lord's resounding "No." We had no vision for what the Lord was doing or where He was taking us, so Monday morning's routine arrived as a welcome distraction from our turmoil. We mindlessly navigated our way through the day preparing for the July 4th holiday, and the kids and I passed the time trying to make the house actually "ours" again.

We were in the throes of trying to enjoy our newly defined existence Tuesday night when the phone rang and Randy excused himself to answer it. Hearing only one side of the conversation, I shook my head in confusion as Matt tried to guess who was on the phone. Seconds later, I heard Randy say his soft spoken goodbye and waited for him to re-enter the room.

Matthew's face was the first to register concern when he looked at his dad, and I immediately felt my self-protected wall rise as I prepared for the news. I cautiously turned to look at Randy and took in his white face and stunned appearance, "What? What is it?" I tentatively asked him.

"I don't believe it," he said, shaking his head in disbelief.

"WHAT?" I asked him again, certain it was time to prepare for bad news.

"Kel, that was the seller asking about the house," he rounded the edge of the door jamb and slowly sat down.

"What about it?"

He went on to explain that the seller of the house we wanted thought perhaps one of the five people who had looked at *our* house on Sunday was her daughter. Not able to connect the dots I asked, "So what?"

"Her daughter thinks she needs to bring her mother by to look at the house…tomorrow."

"Why? She doesn't want to buy another home; she's getting married."

He admitted he couldn't explain it any further, but that was all she said. "I don't get it either but if she wants to come look at it, we don't have any major plans for the holiday. Do we?"

I shook my head no and wondered why in the world someone who is selling her home, who admittedly doesn't want to buy another one wants to spend part of her July 4th holiday looking at this house. Completely bewildered by the whole thing, I shook my head and disregarded the notion with a silent, *Whatever.*

When the seller called the next morning and set an 11 a.m. appointment to see the house, we were like a silent storm quickly trying to restore it back to what it looked like on Sunday. Uncertain as to why the sudden interest in our home, we did the best we could in two short hours and stood by as Randy greeted her at the door. He broke the ice by inviting her on the "Grand Tour" and began showing her each of the bedrooms explaining whose was whose. By the time he led her outside to the backyard, the kids and I chose to stay in, occupying ourselves with another game. Secretly, I kept spying out the window wondering what in the world they were talking about and why was it taking so long. I pretended to be interested in what we were doing, but admittedly it was only a façade. "Mom, your turn," Matt said trying to be patient with my constant delays.

"Oh, oh, sorry," I apologized and rolled the dice, peeking outside rather than watching for what number turned up. "Forget it, you play and I'll watch," Matt said.

The minutes ticked on the clock as my turn led to Anna's, then Matt tried to help Aaron. I looked up again, "They're coming—keep playing."

I listened as the roar of the engine indicated she was leaving and impatiently tried to wait for Randy to come in and explain what that was all about. A hushed thud signaled him throwing his shoes to the ground, then the hum of the garage door closing. "Geez, what's taking him so long?" Matt asked.

I shrugged my shoulders just as Randy opened the back door to the family room. Poker faced—no expression—until he looked at me and broke into a huge smile and said, "You're never going to believe this."

The kids grew quiet... "What?" I asked.

Shaking his head, his smile grew bigger. "I can't explain it and I don't know why, but she wants to buy the house." He threw his hands up, shrugged his shoulders as if to say, "*I don't know*," rolled his head back and laughed louder than I had ever heard him laugh.

We watched him as if in slow motion and waited for his announcement to ricochet around the room before it actually sunk in ... I looked at him, then at the kids, and with an indescribable shriek of delight rejoiced at the faithfulness of our God. Then a holy silence filled the room as we savored the awestruck moment of how it feels when the one true God undeniably and undeservedly moves on your behalf.

Oblivious to anything else in the room, I reflected on my life's journey, marveling at the demonstration of His love for me. *Who are You that not once but over and over again you deliver me from my captivity?* I asked Him. *I did nothing to deserve this yet You have deemed fit to give. Thank You,* was all I could utter as Silence then joined me in relishing all that had just happened.

I rejoiced, then I repented and rejoiced again, for the heavy yoke that comes from disobedience was finally gone, and in its place a spirit of freedom ... freedom to sing and dance and stand in awe of the God I love, for He who promised is able.

It took three weeks—*three weeks*—for us to sell, buy and move into our own personal Promised Land. It was later told to us by a highly successful realtor that the odds of swapping houses are one in a million. We laughed when we heard that for if we didn't know it before, we certainly learned it then: We love and serve a God who constantly defies the odds; He did then and He does now. My life is a testimony to that fact. For although my redemption has been gradual and He has been painstakingly thorough, it has been worth every step He has called me to take.

To Him be the glory forever and ever; He is the only One worthy. Amen.

UPCOMING RELEASES

A Beautiful Restoration

The second in the trilogy, tells the story of God's redeeming power over human fallacy, brokenness and the ongoing account of what grace in action can look like. Woven through the pages of time is one woman's story of God's desire to faithfully reveal Himself in both the joy and sorrow of one's heart. It's a story of life and choice and faith. But most of all it's a story of His great love—a love that consumes not only her life but all of those who come in contact with it.

An Invitation to Intimacy

The last of three in Kelly's inaugural series, *An Invitation to Intimacy* is a poignant account of how God sovereignly uses life's circumstances and setbacks as a means to invite us into our own personal Gardens of Gethsemane, where we once and for all can decide to either lose our life or keep it. Journey through the final segment of Kelly's story as she learns that it is only through the process of laying *everything* at His feet does one truly come to experience the transformational love of the Father.

51125442R10173

Made in the USA
Lexington, KY
13 April 2016